Sex, Your Woman and You:
How to Sexually Please Your Woman in the Bedroom and Beyond

Sex, Your Woman and You: How to Sexually Please Your Woman in the Bedroom and Beyond

By

Don Asterwood

New Tradition Books

Sex, Your Woman and You: How to Sexually Please Your Woman
in the Bedroom and Beyond.
by
Don Asterwood

New Tradition Books
ISBN 1932420754

Contents.

What you can expect from this book.

Whether you're a Wall Street bigshot or Joe Schmo down at the convenience store, every man wants to be a great lover. Every man wants to be a sexual superstar who can leave any woman satisfied and panting for more. Every man wants his lady to think of him as being a stud in the bedroom. This is the one point of pride that every male wants to be able to hang his hat on. Sadly, however, many fall short of this glory. The reasons why some men just aren't that good in the sack are varied. Usually it's just a lack of knowledge, confidence or technique. Or possibly even a combination of all three.

It would be nice not to be the type of man who falls into this category, but if you are, don't give up your loverboy dreams just yet. Hope is not lost. All these disadvantages can be overcome. This book just may be able to help you become more capable in the fine art of pleasing a woman. My goal is to help you develop into a more skilled lover in the boudoir by teaching you the basics of what works and informing you of what doesn't. While everyone that reads it may not become pornstar material, anyone that follows my advice should be able to sexually please their woman.

But before we go any further, let's get one thing straight. If you're looking for a book that's going to show you how to pick up women or get laid, this is not the book for you. If you're looking for a book that's going to show you how to act on a date or find suitable women with whom you would like to have a relationship, then this still isn't the book for you either.

Plain and simple—this book is about showing you what to do once you get a woman or what to do with the one you already have. More specifically, the intent of this book is to help you become more skilled at sexually pleasing your woman. Whether she's your wife, girlfriend or just somebody you picked up for the night, my goal is to enable you to fulfill her needs. In other words, it's about teaching you how to make love to her so that she'll be so sexually satisfied that she'll think of you as a good time rather than a bad memory.

With this book, I'm making the assumption that you already know what intercourse is and what it entails. I'm not going to go into the basic details of insertion and orgasm. I assume that you know this much. What I'm going to do is help you to improve on what you already know. I want to teach you that it's not hard to please a woman. Any one of us has the capability of doing it. I want to tell you what works and how to do it. I also want to explain how some of what you've heard might be wrong and why it doesn't work. And lastly, I'm going to give you other tips that will help you out in the bedroom and beyond.

In order to avoid coming off as too clinical or formal, I will be using somewhat frank and realistic terms in my descriptions of sex and the sexual act. If you're easily offended, take note. While I have done everything to avoid being gratuitously crude or pornographic, I will occasionally be using what some may refer to as "locker room" terms. Please be assured that I have kept these to a minimum and only use them for the purpose of making the subject matter easier to understand. I have found that this is the easiest and most informal way of discussing this subject.

The thing to realize is that if you can sexually please a woman, then you are going to feel much better about yourself and in turn, your woman will appreciate you that much more. Also, when you feel good about yourself, you'll be an even better lover. Which, in turn, will make your woman that much happier. It's exponential. It just feeds itself. And just think about the good time you'll be having pleasing your woman.

Who wouldn't want that?

The importance of sexually satisfying your woman.

When you read the title of this chapter, you're probably thinking, "Is this guy serious?"

Of course I am. This is a very serious subject.

Some of you may think that sexually satisfying your woman merely means that she thinks of you as some kind of stud or something. Well, this is true, but it's only a part of it. The biggest part of it is that when your woman is sexually satisfied, she'll be a much more relaxed and happier person. This, in turn, will make you much happier and your life go much more smoothly as well. And you do want your life to be as easy as possible, I hope?

In my opinion, when a woman is not having good sex regularly, she'll not be quite as agreeable as she would otherwise be. She'll be tense and just generally hard to get along with. This means that she'll probably be more irritated with you than usual and potentially make your life a living hell. You'll probably get on her nerves even more than you already do and she'll probably spend a great portion of your time together griping and nagging at you. It almost seems as though if you can't adequately give her pleasure, then, in her mind, you just can't do anything else right either. There definitely seems to be some correlation in this. I'm sure you've noticed how nice she is to you when you are able to give her an orgasm, right? This is the state you want her in. You want her to be nice to you. To love you and to be relaxed. Sexual satisfaction will definitely put her on the road to this.

Humans are sexual beings. It is something in us that cannot be denied. It is a drive that has to be fulfilled. Sure your girl may get orgasms and sexual satisfaction from masturbation, but that only goes so far. There's nothing like the skin on skin contact of the real thing. When sex goes well, there's nothing better. When it goes bad, you just want to run and hide. If you're giving her more of these run and hide experiences than the toe-curling satisfying ones, then she's probably making your life more difficult than it should be.

Also, don't just look at this as sexually satisfying your lady, look at it as sexually satisfying yourself as well. Not only will you be making your girl happier by providing her with good sex, you'll also be making yourself happier as well. You're a sexual being as well, so not only will her happiness affect yours, but the sexual satisfaction you'll feel will make you feel even better. And this will just feed on itself because the better you feel about yourself, the more you'll be able to put into your lovemaking.

So when you're wondering why it's so important to sexually satisfy your woman, just take a look at your own happiness. When she's happy, you'll stand a better chance of being happy too. While her complete happiness is not contingent on what you do, every little bit helps. Sexually satisfying her will only make things better.

Stop feeling inadequate. You can do this.

If you have any sexual experience with women at all, you're probably acquainted with the sinking, horrible feeling that you get when you've done a less than stellar job in the bedroom. Especially if she's let you know just how badly you've let her down. Whether you couldn't get into it, couldn't get her off or were unable to get it up, it's one of the worst feelings you can have. You were so close to being the sexual commander that you've always thought yourself to be, but once again, you were shown to be just a rank amateur. And even worse, you've disappointed your woman once again. She was a ripe, beautiful flower ready to be plucked, but you just weren't up to the task.

It's just an absolutely demoralizing situation.

What makes it worse is that women can be brutal when it comes to letting us know that we've let them down. They do not mince words in this regard. Some may even question your sexuality if they're feeling especially mean. They just don't understand when things aren't working out for us and we can't get it up. Even though some of the nicer ones may say they do, but really they don't. They can't wrap their heads around the fact that you couldn't take what they were giving. They're just too diplomatic to let you know that while they were expecting a good pounding, all you were able to give them was a mild wallowing.

They act (and with good reason usually) like they've let us into their secret garden of delights and we've had the nerve not to pick the fruit. Or the inability to do so. They don't understand the stress that some men feel when it comes to performing sexually. They think that all men are basically like animals that are just itching to whip it out and stick it in something. Sure some men are like this, but most aren't. Most of us have been taught to be gentlemen and to hold back to such an extent that some women can't handle when reality meets their ideal. Sure they may think that we're supposed to rip their clothes off, but if we actually did that, they might call the cops. Some of us have to be prodded and told what to do. And some women do not like being this dominant in the bedroom. They want to be taken and when we don't live up to their expectations, they feel let down.

But all this is okay. You can bridge this gap. Many opinions that women have of male sexuality comes from movies and dirty jokes. This is probably the same place where many of your ideas came from as well. Once you realize this, you're in the door and on your way to being a confident man in the bedroom.

If you think to yourself, "I've never had any problems in this regard. I'm a real stud," then you're either lying to yourself or you've had very limited experience with women. Or you're clueless to the fact that your woman might be faking it—at least part of the time. Every man has come up short at some point, but this is okay. It's not an ongoing thing. Every problem you have can be overcome. Just don't let it get the best of you.

In spite of all this and whatever hang-ups or feelings of inadequacy you may have, it's time to move on. You can become a great lover regardless of what shortcomings you have. You can *please* her. All it takes is a little confidence and technique. You also have to know how to play to your strengths. Concentrate on what you're good at and improve what you're uncomfortable with. Anything can be overcome if you're willing to put in the work.

Sex is fun. Don't forget it.

A lot of sexual instruction books today seem to forget that sex is a wonderfully fun activity. They are either so clinical they make it cold and inviting or they're so sordid that they make it seem like something that needs to be relegated to a box underneath the bed. They make it embarrassing for more squeamish readers or so boring that you're at risk of falling asleep. They fail to point out that sex is a great way to pass the time and if done right, is guaranteed to be satisfying. There's nothing better to make you feel better about yourself and the world than a good sexual experience.

Regardless, whatever book you read, don't ever forget that sex is about having a good, fun time. It's about enjoying your lover and letting your lover enjoy you. It's about letting go and doing something natural with your lover. It's about enjoying yourself on a primal level.

Another great thing about sex is that the better you get at it, the more fun both you and your lover will have. This will only make the sex that much better because this is a scenario that will grow exponentially.

So don't forget to have fun. Even when you're really concentrating and trying to do your best, remember that sex is about pleasure. And pleasure should always be enjoyable. If you're not having fun with sex, maybe you should rethink your approach.

What she expects of you sexually.

Many men, especially those with little sexual experience, don't really know what their lover expects of them sexually. Should they be dominant? Should they be submissive? Should they be shy? Should they go wild? They are just clueless as to how to proceed. You can see how this can undermine a man's sexual prowess.

The answer to all these questions is an affirmative. You can do all these things in the bedroom. However, you need to remember this caveat: You have to always to be in control of yourself. Regardless of how you start out—whether shy or in charge, you will have to ultimately be in control of yourself and your body. In other words, you are expected to hold out until she is finished regardless of the dynamic.More specifically, you can't orgasm until she's finished or gives you the okay to do so.

But how is it possible that a person can do all these things in the bedroom?

This is a tough one, but I'll explain. You have to be in control of yourself. The basic thing you need to remember (and I'll get into this more later) is that she has been brought up with the idea of defined gender roles. The man is dominant and the female submissive. Even though she may be on top or controlling the situation, physiology dictates that she has to orgasm first—and what this means for you is that you can never get so lost in sexual situation that you forget this. While you can role-play otherwise to your heart's content, ultimately, it will be a situation of the man giving a woman an orgasm first with the man having one shortly thereafter. This is the way it needs to happen if you want to please your woman.

While most women seem to want to let a man control the sexual situation, there are those who like to be in control. They are usually more outgoing and know what they want. This is great for you. Let her do what she wants to you. Just don't forget what is expected of you.

I'm sure that you think that I'm saying that you should fake being something that you're not, but I'm not. Your personality and her personality, as well as the tone of the relationship, should dictate the dynamics of the relationship. All I'm saying is that if you want to please her, you will not lose control of yourself.

The Myths: Why you may be having problems.

I have found that some of the problems that many men have in pleasing their women come from being misled by bad information. Whether it's from dirty jokes, comedy routines, schoolyard talk or some porn movies, some of what you've may have heard regarding sexual performance is probably wrong. I know this personally. When I was younger and had less experience with women, I fell victim to some of this bad information as well. Some things I took for granted as being the correct thing to do in a sexual situation were simply not based in fact. And as a result, I maybe didn't perform as well as I could have. This happens to many men. Especially men who haven't had much experience with women. No one is blaming you or saying that you're stupid or anything because you're not. Unless you have had a lot of experience with women, how are you going to know what's the truth and what's just a punchline?

One of the mistakes that men make is a direct result of something that is sometimes seen in porn movies. It's in how cunnilingus is performed. You often see men going down on a woman and flicking their tongue like they're some sort of amphibian trying to catch a fly. It's like they're trying to mimic a vibrator or something. This is not a very effective technique. Ask any woman. They will prefer a good slow, deliberate licking than a fast flicking any day of the week. A good slow, steady firm licking, like you're eating an ice cream cone, will allow her to get in the groove and come to a bigger and more satisfying orgasm. Just ignore what you've seen in porn and you'll get good results. This one little thing has set men (and women) back sexually for years.

But this is not to say that porn is bad because it's not. You can learn a lot of good stuff from porn. It's is the best way for you to actually see the practical application of sexual knowledge and techniques without doing it yourself. It can also help you become acclimated to a more sexual way of looking at things. Overall, in my opinion, porn is a good thing for couples and individuals to watch. It helps you become more turned on and also gives a good demonstration of sexual acts. But sometimes you have to take a discerning view of what you're seeing. If it's something that doesn't make a lot of sense, it's probably just something that's done to accentuate the visual aspect of this medium.

And while we're speaking of cunnilingus, there's another idea out there that's directly a result of a comedy routine regarding a particular technique. While I'm not going to out and out call this a myth because I've heard some people say it works. However, I've never found it to be true in my experiences. It deals with the idea that one should tongue the letters of the alphabet while he's going down on a woman. I've never met a woman who liked this. They're always like, "What are you doing down there? Stop screwing around and get on with it!" As I mentioned earlier, women prefer a good steady, enthusiastic lick. Like you're eating something you love. There are nuances like how you suck her clitoris and so forth, but it's not complicated. Just stick with the lick and enjoy yourself and you'll see how much she appreciates it. Especially when she starts thrusting against your mouth in orgasm. If you want to experiment with any exotic moves like the alphabet lick, maybe wait until after you've gotten the basics down.

One other myth is that there's a substance (Spanish fly, oysters, green M&M's etc...) that will make a woman so horny that she'll be unable to keep from jumping your bones. This is not true. At least I've never seen anything like this. If it existed you wouldn't be able go anywhere without seeing women humping fireplugs, walls and lampposts. Women like you to treat them well. This is the biggest aphrodisiac of all. They will not have sex with you unless they're comfortable.

Another myth is that a girl who smokes is usually easy. This is true part of the time, but not others. It just depends on the girl who's smoking the cigarette. So the next time a girl bums a Marlboro off you, don't expect her to have sex with you.

And then there's the myth that if you're good enough, you'll be able to turn a lesbian into a straight girl. This is also not true. If she's really a lesbian, this will not be possible. And if you're lucky to get in a threesome or even a one-on-one sexual encounter with a lesbian, chances are she's just experimenting. Or maybe she considers herself bisexual. You didn't turn anyone or anything straight. Just thank your lucky stars that you had this opportunity.

You have to bear in mind that much of what you hear in the locker room comes from guys who probably don't know any more than you do. They're just trying to impress other guys.

There are many more myths and bad information out there, but most of them can be overcome by just using a little common sense and sticking to the basics. Women love sex. At least they love sex when it's performed well. Just keep this in mind and you'll do well. Most stuff regarding sex is just common sense and if you hear something about it that doesn't sound right or seems downright kooky, just look at the source. If this information is coming from somewhere or someone suspect, chances are it's probably suspect information. When it comes to sex, you should be wary of where you get your information.

The double-standard.

Double standards are never good. However, sometimes there's not much you can do about them, especially when it comes to the one between men and women.

Yes, you heard me.

As unpolitically correct as it may be for me to say it, men and women are different. Of course, I'm not talking about in the workplace or any other place where discrimination can occur. I'm talking about sexually. Men and women have different expectations and opinions of themselves and each other sexually.

It is my opinion that women believe this way much more than men. While some men expect women to be feminine, submissive or demure, they're usually fully prepared when a woman is aggressive and sexual. They don't mind it that she likes to show her man who's boss in the bedroom. However, many women are not quite so accepting of such a role reversal in men. Especially when they aren't initiating this kind of play.

What this means is that women expect men to act a certain way and when they don't they may not like it. They expect the man to be dominant, forceful and sex-starved. They expect a man to be ready with a hard-on whenever they feel like having sex. They expect a man to be just a step above an animal in the boudoir. But mostly they expect a man to act like a man.

Accept it. They expect you to be a manly guy. Her idea of what constitutes this kind of behavior will probably have a lot to do with how she was raised and what kind of men she grew up with. She probably expects you to eat a lot, drink beer and be able to fix stuff. The eating a lot and beer drinking may not be a problem, but as to the fixing of stuff, all that is usually required is an attempt at solving the problem. At least try to fix whatever it is that's broken before you call the repairman. She probably won't fault you on your ability but will on your unwillingness to try. The days of the Allen Alda/Woody Allen sensitive/funny guy archetype are over. Wimps are out and will probably remain so. Besides, the only reason why it came about to begin with is because these were the guys who were writing/directing the films. A woman will want a guy like that to help her pick out a purse, but not to have sex with.

Now, this doesn't mean that you need to not be yourself. If you like to cook, cook. If you like to wash dishes, wash dishes. If you like to go shopping with her, go shopping. These are the kinds of things that she'll love. Just let up on the mascara, if you're so inclined. You have to bear in mind that she's watching you. While you may think that plucking your eyebrows is a good thing, she may view it as just a little fruity. Also don't try to play the role as the "masculine guy" because this may throw up a red flag as well. If you try to act too manly and it's out of character, she may think you're trying to convince her of something, you know what I mean? Just be yourself. Just try to avoid doing anything that she might view as too feminine. For example, try not to scream when you see a mouse. If you're not sure of how she views something, maybe feel her out on the subject. Mention that you saw a guy doing whatever it is you're wondering about and then gauge her reaction. If it's okay, do it. If not, then don't. This doesn't mean that you should let her opinion dictate everything you do, but just realize that it may have a direct effect on your sex life.

Of course, sometimes things can be a little more complicated in regards to how she perceives your masculinity. Sometimes, you might have something on your mind or you may be stressed which inevitably causes you problems in regards to your sexual performance. Many women will not forgive you for these faults. While women dream about Prince Charming, in the bedroom they expect a horny caveman. They want to be taken. They want to be satisfied sexually. Your being manly is a big part of this for her.

However, you must also never forget that while she will have and openly express these kind of expectations of how you should act if you are to viewed as manly in her eyes, you will not be allowed to think (or at least express) that you expect her to do things that make her more womanly. Most women see this kind of behavior and thinking as demeaning and sexist. Others see it as downright old-fashioned. This is not fair to you, of course and quite hypocritical, however, this is just the way it is. And if you want to have sex with your woman, you would be mindful to hold your tongue in regards to these matters.

So just bear this double-standard in mind the next time you plan on going on a his/hers manicure date. While it may have been her idea for you to go, she might just be taking points off your masculinity scorecard if you go along. She expects you to be a manly man. If you haplessly pursue activities she views as otherwise, the sexual consequences will be on your head. The same thing goes if you dare suggest that she act a little more ladylike.

She has to orgasm first.

Before I go any further, let me say that I know you're probably not completely unknowledgeable in regards to women. Also I'm sure that you probably already know some of the stuff I'm going to go over. However, I would be remiss not to mention everything that you'll need to know just in case. I don't know your experience. But if you don't know anything about women and everything I'm saying is new to you, it doesn't reflect badly on you. It just means that you haven't had that much experience with females. Not everyone is so fortunate in this area so they shouldn't fault themselves. After all, you have to learn most everything in life whether it's driving, operating a chainsaw or pleasing a woman.

With all this said, let me say that the number one rule of pleasing a woman is that she has to orgasm before you. No if's, and's or but's. As I mentioned earlier in this book, no matter how good it feels or how much relief you need or how horny you are, you have to hold it until she finishes.

The only exception is that she may give you a blowjob or handjob or whatever to get you off before she gets off, however you should never orgasm when she's doing this unless you're one-hundred percent sure that it's okay. And if you're not sure, ask. Never assume anything when it comes to pleasing a woman because this is the number one rule that you must live by.

Sure this is yet another double standard, but you know good and well that most likely if you have an orgasm first, you're going to be done for a while and she's going to left hanging. She's going to be orgasmless while you're lying back spent. She can keep going, but you can't. That's why you have to let her finish first.

Also, here's another rule. Even after she's orgasmed once, make sure she's not going for another one before you orgasm. Remember that women are multi-orgasmic and if you can hold out for her to have more than one, she'll not only be pleased but she'll really think you're a stud.

Of course, there will be occasions when you're going to be so turned on and your girl is going to be so hot that you will not be able to handle it. No matter what you do, you can't hold back. You're a human after all and if you enjoy sex, chances are that you'll sometimes forget and enjoy it a little too much and get lost in the moment. If this only happens rarely, your girl will understand. Especially if you're honest about how turned on you are by her and how you just couldn't hold it. She'll be flattered. Just so long as it doesn't happen that often. If it does, she may just think that you're either selfish or not a very good lover.

And if you do happen to climax first, you have to make sure that you don't just roll over and go to sleep. You have to finish her off. Whether it's with your mouth or her vibrator or your hands, be enthusiastic and make sure that you give her the orgasm she deserves.

As long as you let her orgasm first, you're most of the way there. No woman wants to be left wanting in regards to an orgasm. When you let her climax first it not only shows that you're a considerate person, but it also lets her know that you're a guy who knows his way around a woman.

Her body and yours.

When making love, most women are very turned on when a man caresses their bodies. They love it when they are touched and explored. However, they don't love it when they are pawed and groped.

When you're with your woman, be gentle. Don't grab at her like you're trying to open a bag of potato chips. Take your time and don't be so handsy. She'll love you more and will be better able to get into the sexual act. You'll have fun too especially when you find that your girl is no longer trying to dodge your clumsy advances.

While you need to be gentle and not paw, there is such a thing as being too hesitant. You can't be afraid to touch her. Also, you can't touch her like she's going to break. You have to be firm. And yes, it is possible to be firm without being grabby. If you're shy about how you're touching her, she'll pick up on it and will either think you're turned off by her or that you're so inexperienced that you don't know which end is up. You don't want either of these situations.

The best approach to caressing your girl's body is to start by rubbing her back and move around until you hit all the erogenous zones and then some. The order you go is up to you. Just make sure that you hit all the areas that you find sexy and all the others in between. Be gentle yet firm, rubbing her skin like you're putting on lotion. Don't rush and don't grab. Just feel. You can refer to this as the *Lotion Technique* if it helps you to remember it.

However, you should never linger in one place for too long unless she wants it. A woman wants you to think that there are places on her body that turn you on other than just her breasts and vagina. She wants to be touched all over her body. This includes her arms, stomach, legs, knees, feet and back. Sex is a very sensuous thing and when you touch her in the right way, it will only serve to heat her up even more.

You've heard the term, "feeling up"? Well, this is what you're doing. The only problem with this term is that it has become so associated with inexperienced boys groping girls in the back of their dad's Camry that it's gotten a bad rap. But this doesn't mean it's a bad thing. It is a great feeling when you're properly feeling up a woman, so make sure that you approach it in the right way.

Bear in mind that sometimes she'll want it a little rougher or a little softer than she will other times. This is fine. Let the mood guide you. However, just keep in mind the Lotion Technique and how you shouldn't stay in one place for too long (unless she wants you to) and don't grab. She'll love you if you do these things.

If you can actually get good at properly feeling up your woman, you'll find that not only is she no longer trying to get away from you, but that she's coming closer and making her body more available to you. Humans love skin on skin contact with other humans, your girl is no exception. When you learn to do it right, she'll love you all the more for it.

Know her turn-ons.

If you're going to sexually please your woman, it's a good idea to know what turns her on. This should be a no-brainer, but you would be surprised by how little some men know about their girls.

You can find this out simply by paying attention. Notice what turns her on. Is it kissing her neck? Is it when you kiss her breasts? If you still can't figure it out, you can ask her. Of course you shouldn't be blunt when you go about seeking this information, but you can always start out by talking about the things that she does that turn you on. Most likely, she'll respond by telling you what it is that you do that turns her on. Be sure to pay attention because it is important that you put this new information into play the next time you have sex with her. She'll be happy that you paid attention.

Knowing what turns on your girl is crucial to getting her off. Information is power and the more you know about this subject the better off you'll be. While this is such a seemingly ordinary thing, it is surprising how often it is taken for granted and as a result many men are simply in the dark as to their girls' sexual needs.

The importance of technique.

Some men are less than stellar lovers simply because they don't have a good technique. But when it comes to sex, technique is everything. Enthusiasm and love of sex is important, but if you don't know the basics than you're going to be at a disadvantage.

But what constitutes good technique?

Good sexual technique is comprised of basically knowing the basics and executing them in a competent way. We'll get into the specifics later in the book. But right now, you need to realize that if you can develop a good technique then you will be able to please any woman whenever you feel like it, provided that she is in the mood.

The great thing is that you don't have to be especially well-endowed penis-wise or even have that great of a body to have good technique. It's pretty mechanical for the most part. Just think of what gets you off. Pardon my French, but you can probably jerk off in your sleep and still achieve orgasm, right? This is because you've got the technique down. The same thing goes for women. If you know what to do, you'll achieve results. You will get her off.

As I mentioned earlier, we'll get into to the particulars of specific sexual acts and what basic techniques work later. But for now just realize that you can learn this stuff. Actually it's quite easy. You don't have to be some sort of stud to get your girl off; you just have to know what to do. This is where technique comes in.

Practice makes perfect: Masturbation.

It's simple. The more you do something the better you'll get at it. Sex is no exception. But how do you get better at something that requires another person to participate—especially if that person is not always willing to let you "practice" on her?

Well, you do it yourself. In other words, you masturbate.

I know you've probably been told that masturbation is bad and that it'll make you go blind and other weird stuff but that's all a bunch of hogwash. Masturbation is good and it's healthy. Also by masturbating you'll learn more about your body and gather more sexual experience.

Whoa! Wait a minute? Sexual experience?

Yes, you heard me right. Any sex you have, regardless if it's just with your hand is a sexual experience. This is how you learn. And the more you learn, the better you'll be. And the better you are, the more you'll please your lover. Masturbation gives you opportunities to practice your control so you will be less likely to premature ejaculate. In addition, it'll relieve the tension which will also help you avoid this unfortunate situation. Furthermore, it'll give you opportunities to learn about holding back and not going past the "point of no return." In other words, you're getting a "hands-on" lesson, so to speak, in your personal sexuality.

Now, I'm not saying that you should become the stereotype of the pasty skinned, lonely guy who sits alone in his room, beating it like there's no tomorrow because he can't find a partner. I'm just saying that you shouldn't be afraid to explore this avenue of sexual expression. You shouldn't overthink this. Just do it when you feel like it and learn from it.

Also, I'm not saying that you should masturbate constantly and at inappropriate times. It's a healthy form of sexual expression so there's no reason why you should turn it into something else. Do it at appropriate times and whenever you feel the need. You can overdo anything so make sure that you leave plenty for your woman.

When it comes to learning, there's no better way to learn than to do. Masturbation allows you a pressure-free and enjoyable method of self-exploration and learning about sex. Remember practice makes perfect and sex is no exception.

Too eager to please?

One of biggest faults that some men have as lovers is *not* the fact that they're not willing. In fact it's quite the opposite. They're *too* willing. They're too revved up. They're so happy to be doing it that they lose control of themselves and act like it's their first time every time. They're so excited by the fact that they're actually *doing it* that they get a little too wound up. As a result, they either overwhelm their lady with their enthusiasm or they underwhelm them by getting so excited they either finish too early than or they psyche themselves out and can't perform.

The solution to this problem is simple. Just slow down. You're an adult. You've done this before and if you haven't, try to at least make an effort at controlling yourself. Take a breath and cool it. She'll still be there in a few minutes. It's not like you're on your lunch break and you have only ten minutes to eat a seven course meal. The clock is not ticking. You have to let the situation control the pace. Sometimes you're going to be going hot and heavy and sometimes you're going to be going slowly. Your enthusiasm has to match that of your partner. Just go with it and don't let your excitement get the best of you.

But does this mean that you should play it so cool that you're unenthusiastic? No, not at all. Enthusiasm is one of the greatest tools that you'll have when it comes to pleasing your lady. The idea that you're enjoying yourself enjoying her body is one of the biggest turn-ons for a woman.

However, you just need to not let your enthusiasm get the best of you and be all over her before she's ready. Just take your time, be enthusiastic and let the passion build. That's the point.

But what about quickies? You do the same thing. You have to match your partner's enthusiasm and the mood of the moment. When you're having a quickie, she's in as much of a hurry as you. But that doesn't mean that you lose control. You just let the mood guide the encounter.

The rule of thumb is that sex should never be rushed. You and your partner have to be in sync. If you're going faster than she is, and getting too excited too fast, chances are you're going to disappoint.

If you're unsure about how to proceed, just take a breath and relax. Enjoy your woman. And if she wants to speed things up, she'll let you know.

Enthusiasm: The biggest aphrodisiac.

While it's not important to be overeager, it's also important not to be too laid back. You have to display your interest and passion. You have to show just how turned on you are. And you have to let her know just exactly how much you're lusting for her body. In other words, you have to show just how enthusiastic you are to be with her.

Yes, your enthusiasm is probably one of the biggest and overlooked aphrodisiacs that you'll ever have.

Women love attention. They especially love sexual attention from the man who loves them. They want to be wanted. They want to know just how turned on you are by her. This will feed their passion and make them even more ready to be pleased.

How you do this is simple. You let her know how much she turns you on. You let her know just how hard she makes you. Tell her how sexy she is and how much you want to be with her. Don't be hesitant or shy because she may mistake this as ambivalence. Be somewhat aggressive when you're taking charge of her body. This doesn't mean that you paw her like a piece of meat. However, it does mean that you take command of the situation and let her know what you want to do. You commit to every action you make. When you're kissing her, kiss her with your whole being. When you're sucking her breasts, suck them with all the passion you feel. When you're having intercourse with her, show her your enthusiasm and when she has an orgasm, show her your enthusiasm for that as well. This doesn't mean that you slap her on the back or give her an attaboy. Just be yourself and if you're incredibly turned on by what she's doing, let her know. Now is not the time to play games and hide your feelings from her.

The thing to realize is that your enthusiasm and passion will only serve to feed her enthusiasm and passion. It can be quite infectious. If you act like you don't know what you're doing or that you don't know what you want to do, she'll reciprocate and treat you as such. However, if you let her know how crazy turned-on she makes you, she'll be much more likely to unleash the wild woman inside her.

Premature ejaculation: How to control it.

One thing that stops a lot of men from being better lovers is that of premature ejaculation. They just become too excited too fast and can't keep from orgasming before their partner is finished. And no matter what they do, they can't keep from doing it. It just is something that is more powerful than them and no amount of concentration can stop it. This can be very frustrating to both man and woman in a relationship.

It is my opinion that most premature ejaculation happens as a result of the guy simply getting too turned on. They are hyped up sexually and just get too excited to hold it. A lot of this excitement is caused by inexperience or nerves. There are of course those whose problem is caused by a physical disability. These men should consult a doctor for options. However, if you belong in the former category, your problem can definitely be overcome. I can't guarantee that you can completely eliminate your problem, but unless your problem is medical in nature, I can give you a few tips that may help you in this area.

Tips to help stop premature ejaculation:
- *Wear a condom the next time you have sex.* And if you're a condom wearer, get a thicker one. Or double bag it and use two. You need to decrease your sensitivity. The additional latex around your penis will definitely help reduce the sensation and possibly give you a little more control over yourself.

- *Desensitize yourself by watching more porn.* I know that this one is going to be tough. Just joking. However, some people may have a problem with this, but just realize that the more porn you watch, the more desensitized you'll become. Of course, I'm not saying that you should deaden yourself to sex, but if you're premature ejaculating, you've probably just a little too revved up. If you become a little more immersed in the idea of sex, then you might get used to it and be able to slow down a bit.

- *Masturbate more.* I'm sure that this one will also be a problem. Just kidding again. However, you need to look at masturbation as practice at having sex. The more you do it, the better you'll get at it. Also the more control you'll gain over your body. You need to be able to bring yourself to the edge for long periods without going over. If you do this enough, you'll see good results. I'm not saying that you should be a compulsive masturbator or anything, but if you're ejaculating when you aren't ready, you've probably got a little too much juice built up. You even can tie this one into the previous suggestion if you want.

- *Distract yourself while you're having sex.* You heard me. Focus on your lady, but, as I like to say, put your mind *slightly* elsewhere. Until you've done your duty and made your lady orgasm, think of other things. Just be sure that you don't go overboard and think of something that will make you lose your erection. Try to stay neutral and think of cartoon characters, baseball statistics or food. Stuff you like in a non-sexual way but doesn't disgust you or turn you off. I know it'll be tough especially when your woman really starts grinding against you and panting because she's so pleased with how well you're doing, but you'll just have to stay strong and keep your mind slightly off what you're doing until the time is right.

As I said earlier, most premature ejaculation is, in my opinion, simply a matter of mind over matter and is usually a result of your being too turned on. If you can desensitize just a little, you should see big results. However, if your problem is medical in nature and you can't control your orgasms because of a physical problem, you should consult a physician.

Kissing: A few good things to remember.

While the intention of this book is to get you more knowledgeable about the actual down and dirty act of sex, I would be remiss not to mention the subject of kissing. Or rather what you should remember when you're kissing your girl.

Most women (and men for that matter) love to kiss. It's usually the act that initiates sex. If it's good, things will heat up and the situation might advance to foreplay and from there to intercourse. If it's not, your girl might suddenly develop a headache and leave you hanging. With this in mind, you need to remember that it is not something to be taken lightly. It's fun to do and should progress naturally. It should also come natural to you. You don't need to experiment. It's a very basic act and if you can keep it simple, you'll not only enjoy yourself, but you'll also help ensure that the situation will progress.

The biggest thing to know is that kissing, like sex, is an act of give and take. It's a communication of sorts and the both of you have to in tune with each other otherwise you'll be bumping noses or foreheads. With this in mind, realize that you shouldn't try to jam your tongue down her throat. Unless, of course that she's giving you some sort of signal that this is what she wants you do (which I doubt will happen that often.) Also, don't try to suck her tongue out of her mouth. Some men, for some reason, think that women like this. This is probably because they never get to kiss many women due to this behavior. Remember it's about give and take. Just try to do what comes naturally and match what she's doing and you'll be fine.

Another thing that happens is that lot of men fall short because they just get too excited. As a result of this, they have a tendency to slobber all over their girls. Sure, it's good to be enthusiastic, but while you're probably salivating like Pavlov's dog at the thought of what you're going to be doing to her, keep your spit under control by either swallowing more often or by not letting it run all over her.

Also, if you plan on kissing your girl (and I hope you do), make sure that you brush your teeth often. Don't forget to use mouthwash. You don't want her to taste what you had for supper. This also helps to keep your breath fresh. Needless to say, if you're breath is bad, most likely your love life will not be so hot either. If you can avoid this situation the better off you'll be.

So just remember that kissing is the doorway to experiencing more passion. If you can do it right, you're that much closer to having sex with your girl. If you botch it up, you'll find yourself not only not having sex, but also kissing more than just her lips to get back in her good graces.

Get her in the groove.

One of the most important factors of achieving any orgasm is rhythm. That is to say, the steady motion that allows us to focus and achieve the state that our bodies need to let the sexual act be fulfilled. I know I've used the term, "the groove," a couple of times already, so I thought it would be a good idea to explain exactly what I mean.

When I use the term, "the groove," I'm referring to a rhythmic state of action that allows your lady to concentrate and focus on the pleasure you're giving her and subsequently have an orgasm. This is critical for a woman. And men too, for that matter but not as much. When you're having sex with a woman and you're all over the place, varying your rhythm and what you're doing, she'll most likely have a more difficult time orgasming. She'll be unable to get a handle on what you're doing and will have a harder time getting to a good mental state. I know that variety is the spice of life, but when it comes to sex, leave the variety to the foreplay. If you start doing something that works while you're in the middle of the sexual act, keep doing it and don't stop until she gives you the signal that you should do something else.

For example if you're in missionary position and you're sucking her nipple and she starts moaning from ecstasy, she is effectively in the *groove*. She is in a state where she is focused and is on the road to orgasm. Don't get the idea that you should switch to kissing her feet. Keep sucking her nipple and maintain the rhythm of intercourse. The only reason why you should interrupt this is if you're so excited that you're about to ejaculate. Then and only then can you switch it up, most preferably by giving her a little cunnilingus. Do this only until you get adequate control of yourself and can get safely back to what you were doing so she can get back in the groove.

But how do you get her in the groove? How do you find it? Different things work for different women. The thing is to recognize when she is in it and keep doing whatever it is you're doing that got her there. Some women may like their necks to be kissed while they're having sex. Others love it when you put your hand on the flat of their backs while you're doing it doggie style. It doesn't matter. Just do what works.

People are different so just be sure to recognize when she's there. You can recognize it by keying in to the signals that's she's on the road to orgasm. Since people are different, her signals might not be the same as other women you've been with. However, most likely, they'll follow a usual pattern.

Signs that she's in the groove:
- Increased breathing.
- She's responding well to your movements. In other words she's grinding enthusiastically along with you.
- She tells you that she's about to have an orgasm. (This one should be obvious.)
- She locks her legs around you so you can't get away.
- She's moaning.

You should be able to tell if something is working by how she's responding. But if you can't, you can always ask her. Of course, you can't be blunt, but you can ask in a way that fits into your lovemaking. For example, if you're doing it missionary style, you can lift her legs up and lick her calf. Then say something along the lines of, "Do you like that?" If she does, she'll let you know if she approves.

Of course, once she's to the point of orgasm, it should be easy to recognize when she starts and when she finishes. Some women have explosive orgasms while others will be quieter, but regardless, right before the orgasm she'll probably step up the pace and when she does, you better follow along so she can finish. Remember this is what has to happen before you can ejaculate.

There are a lot of men who think that you should vary things to such an extent that your woman is brought several times to the point of orgasm only to get her release later in a gigantic orgasm. I have no objection to this. That is to say, I have no objection *if* you are an experienced lover and you know your lady well enough to know that she's going to be okay with this. However, since women are multi-orgasmic, some will only see this delay as an annoyance. They can keep orgasming so why do they want to build up to it? But in sex, if it's okay with both parties involved, it's a fine thing to do. Just go with what she wants to do. However, as a novice or a person who is trying to become a better lover, don't try anything fancy. Just get the basics down and get her in the groove so she can climax. I can guarantee that if you do this, there will be plenty of time to experiment in the future because once you can find her groove, it'll be that much easier to get there again.

Remember the groove is a great place to get her to be. If you can get her there, you're home free. All you have to do is keep doing what you're doing and soon she'll be writhing in ecstasy. At this point, it's just up to you to keep up.

Women love sex too.

I'm sure you know your woman pretty well. You know that she likes flowers, little dogs, romantic comedies and small children. However, did you also know that she also probably really likes sex?

She hasn't told you this? Well, most likely she does. And if she doesn't, it might just be because you haven't been living up to your end of the bargain.

But this is going to change, right?

But aw gee shucks, you think. She'll think if I'm some kind of pervert if I act like I'm too comfortable with it.

Don't fool yourself. We're no longer in the Victorian era.

Before you embark on your goal of becoming a better lover, just realize that your woman is a sexual person. Regardless of how your girl may act, or if she is over laden with sexual guilt, she's a human and humans love sex. In other words, she's just like you. She might be a little inhibited or uptight, but deep down she loves orgasms. The sooner you realize this, the better off you'll be.

The reason why I'm telling you this is because many men think that women dislike sex, they are afraid to truly let themselves go because they fear that they'll be judged as being sleazy or deviant because of their sex drive. Don't worry. Because even if your woman does think like this, restraining yourself in the bedroom isn't going to change her mind. She's probably been brought up to think this way about men and probably will always have this expectation. She may act all demure, but all she wants is that orgasm and it's your job to give it to her. And if you're acting all shy and awkward for whatever reason, you're just going to get in the way of what she wants. She's supposed to be the demure one, not you. She's depending on you to get her off and if you don't do it, she's let down. Got it?

But what are you supposed to do?

Put any feelings of bashfulness aside and be the man, so to speak. Just let yourself enjoy the sex because the more you enjoy it, the more she will enjoy it. And in turn this will make you enjoy it even more. There is a connection between two people when they're having sex that is really remarkable. However if one person isn't into it for whatever reason, it can be really uncomfortable for both parties involved. And if you're uncomfortable with your own sexuality or her sexuality, then you're only causing yourself more hardship.

She gets turned on all the time whether she tells you or not. She has dirty dreams and kinky thoughts. She's just like you so don't be so self-conscious and bashful. She might have found these qualities sweet and endearing to begin with, but if you're still doing them on into your relationship, I know that she's just wishing that you would just throw her down and give it to her.

Of course, there are some women who hate sex for whatever reason. Maybe they were abused or were in an abusive relationship, but they are in the minority. If you find yourself in one of these situations, just be patient and don't push. She'll come around if you're a nice guy. She's still human and has needs. She's just been wounded.

So just relax. She likes it. Be yourself. Don't be so self-conscious. Just let yourself make that sexual connection and have fun. Just give her what she wants and you'll get what you want. And if you're too hesitant or timid, you aren't going to get anything.

Use her multiple orgasms to your advantage.

Unlike you, your woman is probably going to be able to orgasm as much as she likes. She may orgasm only once, twice or even several times depending on her mood. Why this is is anybody's guess, but it's just how their bodies are designed. I guess women just got lucky this way. Regardless, the burden is on you. When you're done, you're done. But when she's done, she might just be getting started.

It can be a lot of fun giving women a number of orgasms. You can add sex toys, oral sex and everything else to the mix. If you girl hasn't ever experienced multiple orgasms before, a good way to bring her to this is by using a vibrator. Any one is good, but the more powerful electric ones are the best at this. She may be a little self-conscious at first, but just assure her that you're just having fun and you would love to see her in this way—you won't be lying. Once you convince her that everything is okay and she experiences those vibrator induced multiple orgasms, I don't think you'll have to persuade her again.

You can also bring her to multiple orgasm by intercourse, but this is harder. You'll have a much more difficult time holding back from orgasming yourself. It's best to bring them about by cunnilingus (which we'll get into in the next chapter) or sex toys. You can work on giving her multiples with intercourse after you've achieved a comfort level at giving her that initial one through the other means that I have described.

While it does put more of a burden of her orgasm on you, you shouldn't look at this as a bad thing. It's a great thing for you and will provide you and your lover with a lot of fun love-making possibilities through the use of sex toys, extended cunnilingus and other enjoyable activities. It will be a tremendous turn-on for you and will only make your orgasm that much bigger and better. The most important thing for you to remember is that she can have multiple orgasms so always make sure that she is completely finished before you have yours.

Cunnilingus: The basics.

If you're going to get your girl off, a very important thing you should learn to do is how to properly go down on her. You need to know how to pleasure her with your mouth. This is a basic thing that every man should know and once you get your technique down, she'll beg you for to do it.

As I mentioned earlier, there are a lot of stories surrounding how to perform cunnilingus in regard to different techniques, but I'm just going to delve into the basics. I'm going to teach you how to get her off every time.

The main thing to going down on a woman is to be enthusiastic. Always show that you like it and that you want to do it. Many women are very insecure about "down there" and are afraid that you might be turned off by the odor or whatever. They don't understand just how wonderful it is down there for us and sometimes they have a hard time being convinced with your flattery. It'll take action on your part to show her otherwise. Never ever give the impression that you're squeamish in the slightest bit. She won't be able to get past it if you do. Jump in with gusto and she'll respond accordingly.

And of course, you should realize that you should never just go down immediately. You'll first have to warm her up. You'll probably start by kissing and maybe a little mutual caressing. It's after the clothes come off that you'll want to get started. After things are progressing and you are both becoming aroused, you'll want to get things going by putting your hand between her legs and massaging her clitoris while continuing to kiss her. You can also kiss her breasts and neck. If she responds favorably, she'll probably want you to go further. After she starts getting wet, start going down her chest and her stomach and move down between her legs.

If she pushes you away, just go back to what you were doing prior and don't attempt this again at this particular occasion. However, if she opens up her legs and invites you in, start licking her vagina. Start at the bottom and go up, making sure to lick the clitoris. Pause to suck the clitoris but continue to lick. And here's the key to the kingdom that will always allow you to get her off with your mouth. When you go down on your woman, you'll need to keep your tongue relaxed like you're licking an ice cream cone and keep the rhythm steady. Just like you're masturbating her with your tongue. If you keep a slow steady rhythm, she'll be able to get into the groove and will go down the road of orgasm that much easier. You can also keep rubbing her clitoris with your finger while you're licking her. You can also put your tongue in her vagina but just be sure to keep your rhythm. The biggest part of a female orgasm is the rhythm. If you can keep a steady pace, she'll have one. This is why the tongue flick you often see on porn movies doesn't work that well.

Think about what you like when you're masturbating yourself and apply these same principles to her with your mouth. You're not all over the place with your hand are you? Usually you keep up a steady rhythm in the same place. Just keep this in mind when you're doing anything sexual and you'll do well.

If you're doing things right, you'll soon know and she'll start breathing heavier and moving her hips with your mouth. If she starts doing this, just keep up what you're doing. Now is *not* the time to start experimenting and trying something different. Pretty soon she'll be humping your chin and this is exactly the position you want to be in.

If she isn't responding, maybe step up your pace and be a little more vigorous with your efforts. If she doesn't want you down there, she'll move your head. If she's not protesting your presence in between her legs, it could also be that she actually is responding, but you're just misreading the signals. Just pay attention, it should be pretty obvious is your efforts are being appreciated. Just remember your rhythm and enthusiasm. Don't try to get fancy. Just realize that you're masturbating her with your mouth. If you can keep this in mind, then you'll be able to please her easily.

I know a lot of people have a lot of different techniques in regard to cunnilingus, but this is the only one I've tried that works every time. It's great to experiment with other ones—and I encourage you to do so, but only after you've been able to give your woman orgasms consistently.

The great thing is that once you get her off with your mouth, she'll probably be ready for more. Then you'll be able to have your opportunity to orgasm, but only after you've determined whether or not she wants to climax again.

One thing that I've found that turns on some women is that they love to taste themselves when they're having sex. What I mean by this is that when they're turned on, the taste of their own vagina really kicks things up a notch. It adds just a bit of kink to the situation. You can do this in a couple of ways. One way is to go down on her a little bit before she really gets into and then go back up to and kiss her on the lips. Another way, which is a little more kinkier and even sexier, is to actually put your fingers that you've been rubbing her clitoris with in her mouth while you're going down on her. It's probably good to go with the first technique first to see if she's ready for the second one. Most likely she'll love it. Especially if she's turned on.

Cunnilingus is easy. It's very basic. You're just masturbating her with your mouth. As long as you don't complicate things and stay focused and enthusiastic, you'll have no problem getting her off.

Know your turn-ons.

If you're going to please your woman, it's a good idea to know what pleases you sexually. Sure, it's all about her, but if you're doing stuff that *really* gets you off, your enthusiasm will only serve to feed her ecstasy further.

So how do you find this out? Let's be serious. Surely you know what turns you on. Is it cunnilingus? Do tight jeans do it for you? Is it sexy underwear? Is it doing it in places other than the bedroom? Regardless, if you can figure out what you like, not only will you be really turned on, but she'll be turned on as well.

And how do you let her in on these fantasies/fetishes of yours? Well, that largely depends on the fantasy/fetish. If you're a foot man, worship her feet when you're making love to her. If you like her to wear a particular outfit, suggest it the next time you're talking about things of a sexual nature. She may ask you, "Does that kind of thing really turn you on?" When she does, just be honest and say that you do think it's sexy. Remember the double standard? This will come into play on a lot of these things. She may not find these kind of things sexy at first, but will probably understand that because you're a man i.e. a sex fiend, that it's only natural that something so seemingly mundane/odd would turn you on. Use this to your advantage!

So what happens when she thinks something that turns you on is just a little too much for her tastes? Just let it go. Don't push it. Just laugh it off and go on. It's very likely that when you really start pleasing her sexually that she might just decide to go farther than she has before. That's the great thing about sex. When you're having great sex, you just want to have more and do more. Women are no exception in this regard.

However, there are those of you who may just be a little too kinky for your partner and what turns you on may give her the impression that you're some kind of creep or weirdo. So if you're turned on by unseemly things, you might want to use some discretion in letting her in on this. And by unseemly, I mean potentially unhealthy to you or her mentally or physically. I won't get into specifics, but you should know when something is just a little too dark for public consumption and or might require psychiatric intervention.

But if you're a regular guy, you'll almost certainly have regular guy turn-ons and probably she's going to be somewhat knowledgeable of whatever it is that you may unleash on her. Don't forget that she's in this world too. She's probably not entirely naïve. Just remember that she's a person and she's with you for a reason. She probably likes you a lot. And when you know what turns you on, she'll respond in kind and will be more than happy to join in. Enthusiasm breeds enthusiasm and sexual enthusiasm is no exception.

Don't ever turn her down.

There is one thing that you never want to do to your woman. That is if you want to have sex with her again. Well, okay there's more than one thing that you should never do, but one of the biggest ones is that you should never do is to turn her down when she's wants sex.

Never ever do this. The only excuse that you can possibly have is if you're in a coma or a bodycast. If you do turn her down, she'll be so insulted that she'll probably have a hard time getting over it. In fact, she'll not only be hurt, but will also probably question your sexuality.

This is a harsh reality, I know. But that's just the way it is. Remember the double-standard I mentioned earlier? This goes back to that.

Of course, the main reason for this is that she has probably been brought up to think that all men are sex fiends and are ready to go at the drop of a hat regardless of what's in front of them. Of course, as a man, you probably realize that there is some truth to this, but sometimes you might just not feel up to it. As a result of this kind of thinking, when you turn her down, she's automatically going to take it personally. She's going to think that you have a problem with her and that's the only reason why you don't want to have sex with her.

I know a guy who was dating an attractive girl who was way out of his league to begin with. Well, one night she decided to surprise him by greeting him at the door in the nude. She was *ready.* However, he wasn't for some reason so he said maybe later when he felt like it. The result? She broke up with him the next day. The bright side was that at least he got what he wanted out of the deal. He didn't have to have sex with her. The idiot.

And what if you've just started dating and the girl is ready to take things further sexually than you are? Well this is a case when you're just going to have to bite the bullet and do it. You're going to have to put your chastity belt away if you're going to continue your relationship. You have a small chance that she won't dump you over this, but if you want things to go smoothly, you had just better get down to it. Remember, she's been brought up to think you're constantly in a state of being turned on so when you aren't, she's going to start questioning just what the hell is wrong with you. She is supposed to be the gatekeeper of the sexual part of the relationship and when she gives the greenlight and you don't go, she's going to be irritated. Here she is granting you her beautiful flower and you're saying you've got a headache. Don't be a fool.

And if you're planning on sticking to your guns? Well, maybe this just isn't the girl for you.

So what do you do when she's in the mood and you're not? You get in the mood. You're a man, you can manage. Just realize that you're going to have to step up to the mike and perform. Do not allow yourself the option of turning her down. Just be thankful you've got the opportunity. So many men out there would love to be in your shoes. So if you don't give it up, she might just find someone who will.

Positions: What works?

So which sexual position is the best when it comes to pleasing your woman? Why all of them, of course. That is to say, all of them she likes, that is.

Some women love doggie. Some love missionary. Some love woman astride. Some prefer oral sex. Some love all of them. But usually the reason why they love them is because it's simply easier for them to achieve an orgasm when they're doing it a particular way than it is others.

I'm not going to go into the specifics and graphic descriptions of every position because that is not the intention of this book. This information can be readily obtained in other places. You can watch sexual instruction tapes or view pornography for these kinds of visual representations. Just know that she will prefer some positions to others because they allow her to orgasm faster and experience more pleasure than she would otherwise. The particular positions that enable this easier path to her pleasure will be different for different women so it is your job to figure out which ones work.

The reasons why many women find some positions more exciting and orgasmic than others are varied. For example, she might love doggie style better because she's turned by the deeper penetration or because she loves the way her breasts swing when she's doing it. She might love missionary style because she loves for you to suck her breasts or kiss her while you're having sex. She might love to be on top because she likes to be more in control of the situation and like to grind against you. Or she may love to do it standing up with her clothes on because she just thinks it's kinkier.

You get the picture?

So how do you figure out what works? You pay attention. You subtly let her lead the way a few times. If she's a woman who knows what she wants, she'll lead you down the right path. If not, try to pick up on the cues that she gives you physically. Notice what she responds well to. Take note of those cues and use them to your advantage. If you're doing one thing and she stops you and says, "No, don't move," this is a pretty good indicator that she prefers this position. Women are not that demure in the bedroom. At least not women who have had a little experience. They usually know exactly what they want you to do to them even if they don't come out and say it. And even those who are not that experienced have masturbated and know what gets them off. However, if she's neither type of woman and is unresponsive at all turns, I feel for you. However, don't give up and don't despair. If she's willing, you're almost there. She is a woman and women love orgasms. Just follow these same steps and be patient. Just pay attention to her response and be a gentleman. But you will have to take the lead. It may take her a while to experience an orgasm because she may not know what one is, but after she achieves it once, she'll be a more than willing participant.

Now she may want to experiment with different positions and this is great for you. Just go with it. Sex is a smorgasbord and people like different thing at different times. So just do your thing and get her off.

So what if your girl is not sexually adventurous and always wants to use the same position? Just go with it but gently suggest other ones. She'll come around and want to try new things if she's having good sex and you're pleasing her. A great way that you can get her to go into a different position is to simply start out your foreplay in a different position. If she's a missionary style girl, maybe start by coming up behind her and nuzzling her neck and keep at it with her back to you. You should be able to work this into doggie style. Most women love doggie style, but they have to try it first. You can do this with other positions as well. You can also use this approach to work into a sixty-nine if your girl is into giving you blowjobs. While in the middle of your foreplay and lying down, go down on her with the top of your head towards her feet. This way your penis will be closer to her mouth. If you're hitting the right spots, she'll probably just start giving you head while you're going down on her. If not, just keep performing cunnilingus and try again later. Most likely she'll eventually reciprocate.

But what about what you like? Don't your preferences come into play?

Of course they do. But you have to think of her first. You don't get your orgasm until she has hers. What you can do, especially if she's already a multi-position girl, is to get her off with her favorite position, then switch to yours. For example, let's say that she likes it sitting in your lap with you sucking her nipples and you like doggie style. Get her off the way she likes it and then, after she has orgasmed, ask her to switch positions for you. Mostly likely she will if you have performed well. Being sexual is a big turn-on for women when they're having orgasms through sex. If you're pleasing her, she'll just become more and more adventurous.

Some people have this romantic notion that a couple should be able to orgasm together, but this is foolish and counterproductive (we'll discuss this later in the book). You want to be able to outlast her—by quite a bit if necessary.

She should want this too. Especially if she wants to really stretch her orgasm out or have another one.

So the bottom line in choosing positions is to just pay attention. Notice how your girl is responding when you're engaged in particular positions. You should be able to tell which ones work and which ones don't. Remember this is all about her. You can have a good orgasm regardless of the position. Just be sensitive to her needs and she'll more than reward you in the bedroom.

Intercourse: A few tips.

While I assume you know what constitutes sexual intercourse as far as actual penetration goes (at least I would hope so), I want to give you a few tips on stuff that can help you get your girl off faster in regards to the actual "ins and outs" of the act itself. These are just some basic things that it's good to know before and after you get started.

Don't just ram it in. When you're entering her, be gentle. This is especially true if she isn't completely wet yet. Also, even if she's extremely wet, you need to not be too rough. If she's not completely ready for you and you jam it in, it may be a bit painful for her. This can definitely dampen the mood unnecessarily. So just go easy and gently guide it in in the beginning and everything will be okay

Don't jackhammer her in the beginning. Most women need a little time to get warmed up and if you start thrusting too hard right after you enter her, you might possibly hurt her especially if she's small down there or you're well-endowed. Be gentle at first and then build up the momentum as the situation progresses. Once she's ready, you'll know when it's okay to start cranking it up.

Be enthusiastic but don't lose control. Once things get going well and you're both turned on, be enthusiastic with your thrusting but don't overdo it to the point that you lose control and climax too early. If you get going too fast and find yourself losing control, slow it down or maybe stop for a second and collect your thoughts. Many men think that when they're having sex they should always go flat out. While this may feel good, remember that you've got a duty to perform in giving her an orgasm. Once you so this, then you can pick up the pace.

Another thing that some women love when they're close to orgasming is for a man to just stay still. That's right. They like him to be inside her, still erect, but not moving. He can thrust into her occasionally or stay thrusted into her, but he should not move around too much This allows a woman to thrust and grind against his erect penis as if it was a dildo. It allows her to be in control of the motion because she gets to do the thrusting. This allows her to really focus and can lead to some intense orgasms for her. The guy can start thrusting again once she starts orgasming which will make her orgasm even more intense. If a guy can control himself and pull this off, his lady will love him for it.

These are just a few basic things that are good to know when in the throes of passion. It's easy to get too caught up in what you're doing after you find yourself in the act, but if you can just keep these things in mind, your performance along with your sex life will inevitably improve.

Build her up.

If you're going to please your woman, you're going to have to first get her in the mood. However, if she thinks that she's unattractive or has other self-esteem issues, this is most likely not going to happen that often.

So what can you do?

You need to build her up. Compliment her. Tell her how much you love her. Tell her how beautiful she is. Talk about her sexiness. Tell her what you would like to do with her. In other words, let her know that she is really something special.

If your girl knows how sexy you think she is, she will begin to realize just how attractive she really is. No matter how beautiful they may be, most women have self-esteem issues regarding their bodies and their looks—most likely yours is no exception. So just keep this in mind at all times in your relationship. All you're doing with the compliments is creating a good foundation on which you can build your sexual relationship. If she thinks she's lacking, her issues will just get in the way. You have to realize that females are exposed to all sorts of criticisms of their bodies and looks. They are bombarded by images of gorgeous and skinny models. They see men ogling other girls, while seemingly ignoring them (though they are probably getting ogled too, it's just behind their backs.) You have to remember that most of them are simply starving for someone to tell them how beautiful they look or that they're wearing a great outfit.

But not only should you build her up, you should never do anything to tear her down. I'm sure you're not going to deliberately do this, but even the most harmless comment can be taken the wrong way by a person with low self-esteem. For example, you might want to eat the last doughnut so you say to her as she's reaching for it, "Surely, you're not eating another doughnut?" She may take this as an indirect commentary on her weight, whereas you just want to eat the doughnut. There are many other examples, but I think you get the gist.

Also, when she inevitably asks the question, "Does this make my butt look big?" Your answer is always, "No, you look great." It doesn't matter if what she's wearing is the most unflattering thing you've ever seen. While you know it's the clothing that looks bad, she may possibly think that her butt really is big.

This stuff is really quite simple. Remember flattery will get you everywhere. White lies are good and honesty in regards to how much she turns you on is excellent.

However, as with anything, in regards to compliments, you may want to avoid overdoing it or in a way that she may find insincere or creepy. If you do it too much, she'll think that you've done something wrong and are just trying to compensate. Stay appropriate and compliment when the situation calls for it. Like when she walks by you and looks really great. Tell her how you think. When you're looking at her and you're once again taken with how beautiful she is, tell her. Compliments also during sex are also always appropriate.

When she feels sexy, she'll be in the mood. And when she's in the mood, she'll be much easier to please sexually. She'll not only be turned on by what you're doing, but also by how she feels and by her own body. There's no worse mood-killer than poor self-image.

So build her up. Compliment her. Let her know just how much you love her and she'll feel sexy in no time. And when she feels sexy, your job pleasing her will be that much easier.

Foreplay: Make it your friend.

To some men, foreplay is a four letter word. It's just something that keeps them from getting to what they want—sex. However, if they really know anything about sex, they'll realize that foreplay is not just the prelude to sex, it's actually a big part of it and can be a whole lot of fun.

One complaint women have about the men who make love to them is the fact that they want to jump right to intercourse without properly engaging in all the things they like to do get sufficiently warmed up.

Did you hear me, fellas? Women don't like to just jump into sex. Sure they sometimes are ready to go and want to get down to business fast, but for the most part, they want time to be sufficiently aroused. Now that you know this, you should make good use of this information. If you take the time and give a woman all the foreplay she wants, she'll be much easier to please and you, in turn, will be thought of as a much better lover.

As I mentioned earlier, one of the biggest problems that men have with foreplay is the fact that they separate it from the actual sexual act. They look at it as something they have to do in order to start having sex. Well, this is completely wrongheaded and ridiculously counterproductive. Foreplay is a big part of the sexual act and includes many of the things that you enjoy. Foreplay is by definition what you do prior to sexual intercourse. It includes not only kissing, but also cunnilingus, fellatio, playing/sucking her breasts etc... It is anything that precedes intercourse. This can include even backrubs and a nice, romantic dinner. As you can see, if you really love sex, you shouldn't really have a problem with foreplay. Make it your friend. There's a lot of stuff to enjoy.

Many men also get hung up on the idea that foreplay is just about the kissing. It's not, but let me tell you that this is great place to start. Kissing leads to other things and if you're doing it right, she'll be more than happy to let you do them to her. One thing leads to another and this is why foreplay is necessary and great. Her body doesn't operate the same way yours does. She has to be warmed up and sometimes this can take a little while. She has to have foreplay to have time to get properly aroused.

Here are some tips on a few things to do during foreplay that can help turn her on:

- Kiss her neck. Women love for their necks to be nuzzled.
- Move your hands all over her body. Don't just linger at her breasts or vagina. Her whole body is an erogenous zone when she is aroused.
- Rub her buttocks and back when you kiss.
- Kiss between her breasts.
- Kiss under her breasts. Underneath the breast is a very overlooked erogenous zone. The next time you're kissing/sucking her breasts don't just concentrate on the nipples. Go for the underbreast and you'll be pleased with the reaction.
- Cunnilingus.

A woman will let you know when she is ready for intercourse. When you have done everything that she needs you to do, she'll be more than willing to let you know that she's ready for more. Also, if you've done a good job, you should be able to tell this yourself. If you've sufficiently aroused her, your girl should be wet and ready for sex.

The main thing to realize regarding foreplay is that while you're delaying your orgasm, you're also delaying/building hers up. This means that when she finally does orgasm, it's going to be that much more satisfying. The same thing goes for you. I know it's harder for you to hold it, but you're going to have to learn if you're going to properly please a woman. Remember it's all about her, so the more you can do to enhance and increase her pleasure the better off you'll be.

So the next time before you start to make love to your woman, make an effort to concentrate on the foreplay. Don't just go for the intercourse. It'll only make your life easier if you take your time. Make sure that you've done everything that she needs you to do before you proceed. A woman that has had the proper amount of foreplay is very easy to please. Just bear this in mind the next time you want to jump ahead of yourself.

It's the transition that counts in foreplay.

The problem that a lot of guys have is that they just try to jump into sex. They try to move from kissing their girl directly to intercourse. Usually this doesn't work that well because the girl isn't ready. This is why you need to learn to transition in your foreplay.

Yes, you have to create a smooth break between what you're doing when you're engaged in foreplay. It'll not only serve to get her more turned on, it'll also give her an opportunity to get ready for what's coming next. It's true that one thing does lead to another, however, you can't start in without the appropriate lead in.

The easiest way to transition is by using your hands and mouth. If you're kissing her breasts and you want to go down on her, you simply move a hand down to her clit and start rubbing it while you're still kissing her breasts. Pretty soon, you're moving your mouth from her breasts to her clit. The same thing goes if you're kissing her neck and want to kiss her breasts. While kissing her neck, move a hand to her breasts. Pretty soon you're kissing her breasts.

It's that easy.

The rule of thumb to remember is above the shoulders, the mouth leads the hands. In other words, use your mouth primarily above the shoulders. Below the shoulders, the hands should lead the mouth. In other words, caress before you kiss anything other than her lips or neck.

As for intercourse, usually the penis will follow the hands and mouth both above and below the neck, but there will be occasions when the order of operations will be thrown out the window, especially with oral sex. Usually vaginal and anal penetration will always follow manual and/or oral caressing.

Of course, there will be exceptions to this as you get more and more skilled as a lover, but this is the most basic way to start. Also, as your sexual relationship progresses, there are times when she'll just jump from one thing to another and that will be okay as long as this is what she wants. However, when you're driving things, it's a good thing to keep the idea of transitioning in mind.

Go with what works.

You've heard the old saying, "If it ain't broke, don't fix it?" When you're making love to your lady, this same phrase applies.

Huh?

In other words, when you're doing something right (and you're sure that what you're doing is turning her on), keep doing it until she either has an orgasm or you feel that it's okay to move on to the next thing. This will please your woman more than anything.

This is a very similar idea to getting her in the groove. However, this applies more to generally making her feel good so that you can get into the groove. After all, how is she ever going to get into the groove if she's so off balance from your unfocused efforts that she doesn't know what's coming next?

Basically all this entails is that when you're doing something that works, keep doing it. If you're kissing her neck, keep kissing her neck. If you're kissing her breasts and she's responding well, keep doing that. I'm not saying that you should do only this, but linger on what feels good for her. This will cause her to become even more turned on. The problem some guys have is that they switch things up too much and never allow a girl to get into the groove. They are kissing her neck one second and then going down on her the next. And twenty seconds after that, they're sucking her toes. She never knows what's coming and can never truly enjoy sex this way.

As for moving on to the next thing, just go with your gut. If she's getting off by you kissing her neck, you can tell when she's ready for something else. It's the transition that matters. For example, you're kissing her breasts and she's really getting into it. Next you can try putting your fingers on her clitoris and rubbing it while continuing to kiss her breasts. Then you can easily transition into cunnilingus, but you didn't just jump to it. You kept doing something she liked and then started doing something else she liked.

So, when you're doing something right. Keep doing it until it's time to move on. If you stop doing something that's right, most likely you're going to be doing something that's wrong. Just bear this in mind.

Navigating her erogenous zones.

If you're going to sexually please your woman, it's a good idea to get an idea about her erogenous zones. This is to say, it's a good idea to know what parts of her body are her turn-on points. I know that most of these are common knowledge, but there are places on a woman that you probably didn't even think were erogenous zones.

Here's a list of the most common erogenous zones:
- Breasts
- Neck
- Lips
- Neck
- Legs
- Butt
- Stomach
- Clitoris
- Vagina
- Anus

And here are some of the less common ones:
- Knees
- Feet
- Shoulders
- Lower back
- Armpits (yes, armpits)

These are the places that your girl will love to be touched and caressed. These areas are the places that will make your girl come alive with lust. Respect them and know them and they will unlock your girl's libido.

Of course, each woman is different and will have different erogenous zones. She may be more turned on when you touch her knees than she is when you touch her breasts. Or she may even be turned on by something completely different. She may even love for you to touch her hands. However, these individual preferences will be something that you'll learn about your girl in your sexual explorations.

One thing to realize is that your girl may not even know that she'll be turned on by some of these places. If she's never had her lower back caressed, she may not even know that it turns her on. So, don't assume that just because you've never kissed her feet that she doesn't like it. Just try it.

How you approach these erogenous zones should be commonsense. You should approach them sensually. You should caress them. You should never grope, paw or slobber. You should kiss them and you should worship them. While you may not necessarily get a kick out of licking your girl's armpits, she may love it. Remember this isn't about you. It's about her and what turns her on. The more she gets turned on, the easier it will be to please her. This means there's less pressure on you and this means the more fun you'll have. If your girl likes what you're doing, she'll let you know. If not, she'll let you know that too. Remember to transition.

Also, you don't want to be too eager for one part of the body, at least not until you know that your girl likes what you're doing. This might make you seem a little bit weird if she's not used to this out of you. You don't want to come off as a fetishist. That is unless you are a fetishist, of course. And if you are, it might be a good idea to keep this under wraps at least until you know that she's okay with your fixation.

As I mentioned earlier, some of these erogenous zones are fairly common knowledge, but some aren't. All of them may not apply to your girl, but most will. Be familiar with them and try caressing a new one each time you make love to your girl. Don't take the shotgun approach and do them all in one session, but mix it up and try a different one or two each time. Don't be obvious about what you're doing, just try a gentle caress. If your girl responds well, you're onto something. If not, try something else. Remember variety is the spice of life and your girl will love the fact that you've discovered new parts of her body that turn her on.

Anal?

Anal sex is a subject that at one time was pretty taboo, but is now fairly common. It's a form of sexual intercourse that a lot of guys want to try with their girl. A lot of girls want to try it too, it's just that they're either afraid of the unknown or don't know exactly how to get started. It's also something that a lot of girls never think they would like but absolutely love once they do it.

The fact of the matter is that it's not that hard, especially if both parties are willing. However, that's the problem. Usually it's a case of the guy wanting to do it, but the girl is hesitant. If this is the case, I can give you a few tips on how to get her in the mood for anal play.

The thing you need to realize is that you have to work into it. You cannot just start trying to jam your penis in her anus. This will not only be painful to her, but will also probably be painful for you as well. You have to warm her up to it and how you do this is easy. I've found the best way to get a girl warmed up for anal sex is to transition it from cunnilingus. When you're performing oral on your girl and she's good and wet, put a finger in her vagina. Work with it until your fingers are good and wet. Then while continuing to lick, move your fingers to her anus and begin rubbing it. Most likely, she'll respond favorably especially if she's very turned on. The anus is a major erogenous zone and she'll love for you to rub it. If she responds favorably, try gently and slowly sticking a finger in. It may be a bit difficult, especially if it's the first time. She may have trouble relaxing. However, don't force it. If it's too difficult, just abandon this idea and go back to rubbing again. However, if she's wet enough, especially if this wetness is extending down to her anus, you should be able to work a finger in without too much effort. Once you're in, try inserting your finger just a little bit and if it's going well, try another finger. She should love this. If not, go back to one finger. I hope you can see the pattern here?

Once she's enjoying more than one finger, she's going to be prime candidate for anal sex. She may ask you to enter her anally, and if she doesn't, ask her, "Do you want to try doing it this way?" If she says yes, then great. If not, don't push it. Just continue what you're doing and consider it foreplay. But if she's ready, you need to keep in mind that you will probably not be able to enter as easily as you do her vagina. It may take some effort and a lot of lube. You have to be careful and put it in slowly because it may be a little painful, especially if she tenses up, for her until you get it in. Once in, you might want to take it easy and follow her cues. If she wants it faster, do it faster. If she wants it more gently do it more gently. Whether or not you orgasm this way is up to you, just don't forget that she has to orgasm first. And she very well might this way.

One big thing to keep in mind is that while it's quite sexy, anal sex can be a little, ahem, for lack of a better word, *messy*. So be prepared. Also never put your finger or penis into her vagina or mouth after it has been in her anus. This can very unsanitary and could possibly cause her health problems. Condoms are especially recommended for anal sex because of the likelihood of the tearing of the rectal wall during sex. This can make both you and your partner more susceptible to disease and sickness.

Please bear in mind that some girls will not like the idea of anal sex and there's nothing you will ever do to convince them otherwise. If this is the case with your woman, just don't worry about it. It's not worth the hassle. If she's dead set against it, you'll never be able to convince her of it. If it's something that you really want to do, just hope that she'll have a change of heart. But bear in mind that this is not a topic that you should keep bringing up especially if it's offensive to your girl.

Anal sex can be great. Whether your girl likes it because of the naughtiness of it or because of the feel, you'll have a good time regardless. You just need to go at your girls pace and be sure that you remember your order of operation.

How to last longer: A good way to practice.

A lot of guys are not necessarily premature ejaculators, but would like to be able to last longer and develop more control of their orgasms. This is a great aspiration and only helps you in your quest to sexually please your woman.

A good technique that will help you last longer is that when you masturbate either by fantasizing or watching porn or whatever else gets you off, instead of bringing yourself to orgasm, bring yourself to the *point* of orgasm and then let off. Do this as much as you can stand it. It'll be tough at first, but eventually, you'll find yourself developing control of your body and your orgasms. The longer you last will not only increase the amount of pleasure you give your girl, but also yourself as well. A delayed orgasm will only be bigger and more powerful for you.

Orgasming together?

I know you've read the novels and seen the films. A couple is that is truly made for each other orgasms together, right? It's the ultimate sign of sexual compatibility, right? It just shows that you were made for each other, right?

Wrong.

Yes, you read right. Sexual compatibility has nothing to do with your ability to climax together. Sure, it's a nice idea, but it's not really true or even that desirable. You don't want to orgasm at the exact instant she does. You want to hold out until you're sure she's finished and then some. You want to be able to orgasm whenever you know it's absolutely okay or when she wants you to.

Yes, it's true. Once again. She orgasms first.

If you climax at the exact instant she does, most likely she's not completely through. You want to hold out so she can finish grinding it out. She may still have another one in her that she wants to work out as well. So if you're finished and she's not, she's not going to very happy.

Even after they've orgasmed, most women like to continue thrusting against you for a little bit. It just lets them work out the remainder of the orgasm and really hit a good level of satisfaction. However, if you're deflating, it's just not going to be as good of an experience for her. Not to mention, if you're using a condom, you have to pull out as soon as you're finished to get the full benefit of its prophylactic qualities. It'll possibly leak otherwise.

Sure there are going to be times that you will be unable to help yourself and will not be able to hold out, but make these the exceptions rather than the rule. Also there are going to be times when she'll want you to orgasm with her. When this happens, do it. Remember you're pleasing her and if this pleases her then good. Most likely she'll want you to hold out just a little bit longer to allow her full satisfaction.

So while it's a romantic notion, just put it out of your head. Your job is to provide a good platform for her get off. If you finish before she's *completely* done, it's almost as bad as if she didn't finish at all.

Porn/erotica as aphrodisiac.

Of course porn turns you on. Everybody knows that, you think. However, it's the idea that it can help you enhance your lovemaking that's the concept that you should embrace. This is because the more the two of you are aroused, the more pleasure you'll have sexually.

Pornography by its very nature is designed to raise your libido. This is only natural and there's nothing wrong with it. It doesn't make you a pervert or scumbag for watching it. It only means that you're a human. Sure such stuff is not usually for mainstream consumption, but then again this is not to say that it isn't consumed on a mainstream basis. Almost all adults are familiar with porn and almost all adults have viewed it at some time or other. The same thing goes for erotica. It's just a different manifestation of the same thing. The only different is that you watch one and read the other.

Try to incorporate either of these into your love life by watching it with your significant other. It'll not only heighten the mood but will also give your libido a boost. While erotica is more of a solitary pursuit, this can be overcome by sharing the book. Or by reading two different stories independently of each other. Porn however can be viewed together.

Most likely, if your girl is thoroughly modern she won't have a problem with porn. However, you might want her to share in the choosing of it. She may have a different idea of what is a turn-on than you do. Cater to this and be glad that she's participating. I can assure you that because her arousal is being increased as a result of her participation you probably won't have a problem with what she picks out.

However, if your girl is a little repressed, you may want to ease her into it. You can suggest it at an appropriate time like when the subject is on the TV or when you see a magazine article about it. Just say something like, "Why don't we watch one of these together?" If she agrees, wonderful. Then the both of you should pick it out. Don't already have one planned. She needs to feel like she's just as involved in the process as you. Also don't act too eager to do this. You don't want her to get the wrong idea that you just want to watch a porn movie. Remember the double standard? Well this also applies to porn. Most likely she's been taught that it's dirty and perverted, so just bear this in mind. Sure she wants to watch it, but she'll probably subconsciously form an opinion of you if you're too gung ho. Just remember to play it cool and you'll be all right.

However, if she doesn't respond favorably after your proposal of watching the film together, then says something along the lines of, "Why would I do something like that?" or "What are you? Some kind of pervert or something?" Just laugh it off and let it go. Don't push or try to defend yourself. Just say something like, "I just thought it might be a fun thing to do together," or if she reacts too harshly, give her the old, "I was just joking," routine. Regardless of which way you choose, just let it go. You've succeeded in planting the seed of this in her and the next time you bring it up, she may react more favorably. Just be sure not to do it too soon or at an inappropriate time.

And what do you do once you're watching? You just let nature take its course. Sit together and let the foreplay begin.

Soon enough during the course of the movie both of you will start to feel it and just let the good times roll from there.

However, bear in mind that you know your girl best. If you know beyond a shadow of doubt that she'll most likely dump you or something for even mentioning the idea of watching a porn movie, it's probably a good idea to avoid doing this. Erotica might be a better option. Many times people will read smut when they won't watch it. But some women are even too uptight for this. If you have a good feeling that this is the case, you may have to either abandon this course of action entirely or take a different approach. Maybe you should just suggest a sexy movie. Something that's sexy but can be shown on regular TV. The subject of porn can be a little touchy with some women. Some women even regard watching porn as a form of cheating. This is extraordinarily weird but it's true. So tread lightly if you think your lady is on the ultra-straitlaced side.

If you're in the majority, which most likely you are, your girl will like porn and erotica. Everybody likes to be turned on and she'll be no exception. And when she's turned on she'll be easier to please and she'll have much more fun when she's having sex. This is the point because the more her libido is boosted, the easier she'll be to please. Whether it's by the both of you reading/sharing erotica or by watching porn, the more turned on the two of you are sexually, the better time you'll have.

Impotence: How to deal with it.

I know it's a subject that many men don't want to acknowledge, but it's something that can happen to anyone. It doesn't matter how virile or how studly you may think you are. When you're in the middle of things, anyone can experience this, ahem, ego deflating problem.

Now I'm not talking about actual medically diagnosed impotence, I'm referring to the occasional bout that you'll probably experience at least once in your sexual lifetime. The fact that it's so random is what makes it so hard to deal with for so many men. It can just really bring you down and make you feel very inadequate. The thing about sex is that you're really only as good as your last performance. So if you let your girl down, it can really be a big deal.

But it shouldn't. If it's not a regularly occurring situation, it's really not that big of a deal. It's normal and happens to everybody. Remember nobody is perfect and just like there are times when you can't focus on other tasks, there will be times when you can't focus on sex. This is when problems occur.

Aside from a physical problem, the reasons why you may experience this problem are many. It could be that you're stressed. It could be that your mind is on other things. Maybe you're drunk. Maybe you've been smoking too much. It could even be that you're trying so hard not to premature ejaculate that you've distracted yourself too much. You also just might be too turned on so much so that you psyche yourself out. Regardless, it can be humiliating when your girl is there waiting and ready and you're not up to the challenge.

So what can you do?

The most important thing is to not panic. Panicking will only make it worse. This is a problem that feeds on itself. If you're scattered and stressed in your thinking, you'll just make things go downhill even faster. Remember this is what got you in this position to begin with. If you can relax and get your mind straight again, your erection may come back. If you can just relax, you still have a shot. Prolong the foreplay. Perform cunnilingus with even more gusto to get into the mood again. And if things are too bad, suggest taking a break. It's better to not even start if you're not going to able to finish it.

The next thing you can do is to apologize to your lady. Assure her that it's not her and that she is very sexy and you're exceptionally turned on, it's just that you're experiencing a little physical difficulty. Women can be very hurt and insulted when a man can't get it up. They automatically assume that it's their fault and that you're repulsed by them or something otherwise you would have a raging hard-on. Remember the double-standard? It's in full effect here. You're expected to perform regardless of what's going on in your life because you're basically just an erection on legs. She can have a headache if she's not up to things, but not you. You're expected to be ready and feeling it all the time. This is why she will be probably be insulted and hurt. So anything you can do to assuage these feelings in her will be good. You have to remember that she probably won't understand just how badly you feel about it—how you feel probably much worse than she could ever possibly feel. However, if you show your remorse fully, she'll probably give you a pass.

So the bottom line is that it happens to everybody. No matter how much of a stud you may think you are, you're still prone to this problem. The key is to relax and not make too much of it. Because there's not really that much to think of it. It's just something that can sometimes happen. And if you keep having this problem, it might be a good idea to see a doctor. You may have a physical problem.

Confidence.

Women love confident men. And they especially love men who are confident in the bedroom. This being said, if you're a confident man in the bedroom, you're going to be a better lover. And if you're a better lover, you're going to be more likely to please your woman.

So why do women like confident men? You remember the double standard? How they're always looking for Prince Charming to have a relationship with, but want a caveman in the bedroom? While they may be liberated women, they want a man who will take charge in the lovemaking. They want a man who will set the pace and drive the process. They want a man who knows what he's doing. They were brought up to be demure ladies so it's going to be harder for them to lead when it comes to sex.

If you're unsure of yourself or act like you don't know what end is up in the bedroom, your girl will pick up on it. If she has to lead the way because you don't know what to do, she probably isn't going to like it very much. Sure there's the fantasy of the older woman as sexual teacher, but just realize that this isn't the way things usually work. Most women, even those who are sexually dominant, want their men to be confident even when it's the woman who's in charge.

So how do you become more confident? This is simple. You have to fake it until you make it. Pretend to be confident until you are more confident. If you're not sure how to go about this, observe someone who you perceive to be confident. It can be someone in real life or someone in the movies. Use this person as a guide and model his behavior. You can also roleplay as someone who is a confident lover. If you do this enough, pretty soon, you'll find that you are a more confident person and a better lover and since this feeds upon itself, you will soon find yourself growing even more confident.

However, while you should be confident, realize that there is a fine line between confidence and arrogance. Try not to cross it. You will do this if you do any of the following:

- Brag about how great you are in bed and/or how wonderful you are in general.
- Strut around like a rooster
- Be rude or cocky.
- Act too smug after sex.
- Boast about your conquests.

The best thing you can do is exude a quiet confidence. That is to say, act like you are *the man* without telling everybody that you are the man. If you act confident, everyone will know just how great you are soon enough.

Confidence is a great quality to have when you're trying to please your woman. Try to cultivate it however you are able even if you have to pretend at first. The goal is to get your girl off and if you're some sort of bumbler, even if you fundamentally know what you're doing, you're only going to make her wince at your attempts to please her.

Her breasts: What she likes.

If you're like most guys, you're probably at heart a breast man. I know that some guys love legs, some love faces, but universally we all love breasts. Whether they're small, big, gigantic or pert, all varieties of women's breasts have their fans. Some of us love all kinds. I know I fall in this category. However, while the spirit is there, a lot of us lose ourselves in our enthusiasm. We get so hyped up that a disconnect occurs in how we act towards our lady's breasts and the way that she would prefer we act. We just get too rough in our lust for them. And believe me, if you're too rough with your girl's breasts, you're not going to help your cause.

But this is a problem easily fixed.

The key is to be firm but gentle. Play with them, but don't paw them. Suck them but don't give them hickies. And bite them only gently. Never chomp down. In other words, treat them the way that you would have her treat your penis. Like you're happy to have your hands on them and you're not afraid to touch them. Like you're handling someone else's body, which is indeed what you're doing.

The great thing for us guys is that women love for their breasts to be played with. It is one of their major erogenous zones. They love for us to suck and play with them. All you have to do is treat them right and she'll treat you right.

As for what particular parts of her breasts give her a turn-on, this is simple. They're the same parts that turn you on. She loves for you to suck on her nipples and to lick her breasts. However, there's one part of her breasts that is usually overlooked by most men. This is underneath her breasts, the part below her nipple that connects to her chest. This part of her breasts rarely has any attention paid to it, but is a very erogenous zone. The next time you're with your girl, spend some time licking and fondling her underbreasts and she'll respond favorably.

Another tip in breast play is to gently bite her nipples at the moment she orgasms. Don't hurt her, but just gently put your teeth on them and press down without inflicting pain and it'll only heighten her orgasm.

As for what some guys refer to as *tit-fucking*, this is a matter of personal preference on the part of your girl. While almost all guys love this, some girls may not. However, many do. They love the attention and the erotic nature of the act is a big turn-on. It can be great foreplay leading up to vaginal intercourse. However, never assume that your girl wants you to do this. Always ask. If she doesn't, fine. Don't push it. The same thing goes for orgasming on her breasts (only after she has orgasmed, of course). Always ask. Some girls like this. Others don't. If she says yes, be courteous and try not to squirt anywhere other than her breasts. If you get it in her hair, she won't be too happy with you.

Women's breasts are wonderful things. Pay them the respect they deserve and she'll not only love you for it, but will also look more forward to making love to you.

Etiquette for blowjobs and how to keep getting them.

If you're like most men, you love for your girl to give you head. You love for her to go down on you. And if you're like most men, you probably think your girl doesn't do it nearly enough.

Well, there are probably reasons for this.

Many guys are just not considerate when it comes to getting head. They act like when their girl is giving it to them, they have to make the most of it because it's never going to happen again. And when guys think this way, it usually doesn't.

The thing about it is that most women don't mind giving head. In fact, a lot of them love it, it's just that guys ruin it because they're too eager and just blow whenever and wherever they feel like it. They assume that just because a girl is giving them head that she's ready for the whole porn star swallowing experience. Many women are not. They just want to get you aroused and ready for intercourse. Don't assume anything. Remember the rule about not orgasming until she does? It still applies here.

If you want your girl to go down on you and to keep going down on you, you need to observe some basic rules. This will make the experience much more pleasurable for her and you'll be less likely to run the risk of completely pissing her off.

Here's what you should and shouldn't do:

Be a gentleman. As with any sexual encounter, you'll go much farther and be more likely to have sex more regularly if you're on your best behavior. Consideration is the key. Don't treat her like she's there just for your pleasure. She's getting off too when she's giving you head because the idea of what she's doing to you is a turn-on. Don't ruin it by doing something that she doesn't want.

Don't orgasm until you're sure it's okay. This one should be obvious but I'll explain it anyway. You should never orgasm until you're sure your lady is ready for you to. This means to wait until she gives the okay. Just because she's going down on you doesn't necessarily mean that she wants to give you an orgasm this way. She may be looking at it as foreplay. She may just be getting you good and hard for intercourse. So before you climax, make sure that you let her know that you're close. Remember that once you're finished, you're done for a while. You don't want to leave her wanting. This will give her adequate time to let you know what the plan is.

Let her know when you're close to orgasming. This is just being considerate. This will give her the time to get away, to slow things down or to clamp down and give it all she's got.

Don't ejaculate in her mouth before you know if it's okay or not. One thing that women hate when giving head is for the guy to take it upon himself release himself in her mouth. Be a gentleman and don't assume she wants this. This may not be her thing. Always let her know when you're close so she'll have adequate time to get ready. Either she'll remove her mouth or she'll continue on. Regardless, it's her choice not yours.

Don't ejaculate in her hair. This one should be obvious. Sex can sometimes be a little messy but don't assume that just because she's giving you head that you've got the license to ejaculate wherever you feel like it. Sure, accidents happen, but try to take care not to ruin her hairdo.

Don't ejaculate on her clothes. The same rules apply as above. Don't ruin her outfit just because you're trigger happy.

Don't force her head onto your lap. If you're considerate, you'll let her come to you. There should be no need to be so blunt about what you want. If your girl wants to go down on you she'll do it without you guiding her in.

Don't criticize her oral sex skills. If you want her to stop giving you head permanently, this is a good way to start. She's doing something special for you and will not take your criticisms lightly. If she's doing something you don't like, gently suggest that she do something else. Like if she's biting the head of your penis and it hurts, instead of telling her that she's causing you a lot of pain, gently ask her to lick it instead. Everything is in how you say it. Criticism of your girls oral sex abilities are no exception.

Praise her efforts. While she's doing it, let her know what a good job she's doing. And after it's over, let her know how much you appreciate what she did for you. Even if she didn't do that great of a job, act like it was the best. This way, she'll do it again which will give her ample time to improve. Everybody likes it when people aren't taking them for granted.

The key to getting oral sex is consideration. The more considerate you are of your girl, the more likely you'll be to get head. Would you like it if you didn't have any clue what you're girl is going to you when you go down on her? Just put yourself in her shoes and you'll be alright.

Does size matter?

Let's face it. A lot of guys have a lot of insecurity about their penis size. Just check the spam in your inbox if you don't believe me. If this wasn't true, all ads for penis enlargement treatments, pills and contraptions would cease. The thing about it is that most guys, unless they're hung like horses of course, would like to be bigger in the pants. While a guy who's got five inches would kill to be six, a guy who's six would kill to be seven and on up the ladder.

But does size really matter?

I'm not going to lie to you. To some women it is an issue. But to most it is not. Most women are interested in your personality and the overall feeling they get from you. And most likely you are big enough for them. They're with you aren't they? Since they're in a relationship with you, you've probably passed the personality test. Besides most women aren't that hung up on penis size in regards to sex. Sure they may think a big penis is nice to look at or fantasize about, but the thought of putting anything too big in them isn't that appealing to them. In fact, it can even be downright uncomfortable.

As for the women who make the biggest issue about penis size are what are referred to as *size-queens*. They are usually fetishists. Big penises are their thing and they don't really care who is it's attached to. The actual guy doesn't matter, because it's all about the sex. Men are just objects to them and if you aren't packing, then they aren't interested.

And if you've had the misfortune of being rejected on these grounds alone, try not to take it too personally. At least you found out early on what these women were about and didn't have to waste too much of your time.

So how can you please a women if you're not so well endowed? You need to play to your strengths and stop feeling so inadequate. You need to realize that because a guy is particularly gifted in the trousers, he may not be that great of a lover. This is probably because he's never really had to work at it. All he has to do is show up. This can make him rather one-dimensional in regards to love making. This is why you need to work on your basic skills. Know how to properly perform cunnilingus. Know how to properly treat a woman. Know how to compliment. Know how to hold out until she is thoroughly satisfied. Work out and make your body look as good as it can. It's all these things that make up a good sexual experience not just the size of your penis.

And if you're lucky enough to be on the large end of the scale? Congratulations. But just don't leave your sexual ability at that. If you can work on your skills in other areas, then you'll be unstoppable in the bedroom. Take advantage of your gifts and work on your basics to be the absolute best that you can be.

Size may matter to some, but that is not the whole of it. It doesn't matter how big you are if you don't know how to use what you've got. And if you know how to use what you've got, it doesn't really matter how big you are. There's a lot more to sex than how deeply you can penetrate her.

Play to your strengths.

The problem a lot of guys have when they try to please their ladies sexually is that they do not play to their strengths. They lack self-awareness as to what they're good at sexually and as a result spend time doing things that may not necessarily be their strong suit.

So the next time you have sex with your girl, pay attention to yourself. What are you good at? What are your assets? Find them out and use them to your advantage. Do you have a big penis? Well, then use that. She'll love it. Can you last a long time? Use that and give her a long hard ride. Are you good at cunnilingus? Get her off with your mouth. Do you have a good body? Show it off for her.

This stuff is simple. While it's essential that you be well-rounded in your sexual technique, it's also important that you know what you love and what you're good at. Sure, you should work on any weaknesses you have, but remember to always play to your strengths and use them to your advantage. She probably already knows what you're good at and probably wants you to concentrate more on this stuff. If you can just figure it out too, you'll have it made.

Sexual guilt.

Whether it's because of lack of knowledge, experience or even physical ability, some of you are just going to come up short when it comes to pleasing our women. But sometimes it's not because of any of these reasons. Sometimes it's because it's somehow ingrained in you that sex is a bad thing. Some of you think that it's "dirty" or "vulgar." You think that it's nasty and feel guilty when you think sexual thoughts or want to engage in sexual behavior. You feel that being sexual is wrong, regardless of the fact that you're in a committed relationship or married. You feel horrible for looking at pornography and scold yourself for masturbating. And after you're finished with the sexual act with your significant other, you are ashamed regardless of how much you were into it while in the process. You think that sure it's something necessary to procreate but it's not exactly something that you should act like you really enjoy. Even though you really do.

If you feel like this, it's probably because at sometime in your life, it's been drilled into you that sex is wrong. That it is a sign of moral decadence. You may not even realize that this is what is hamstringing your efforts. The problem is that some people can't accept the fact that something that is so wonderful can possibly be a good thing. They think that because the subject of sex is involved that it can be nothing other than sleazy. Also even if you do not initially feel this way, those who do feel this way can force their own small-minded repression onto you and as a result will corrupt your way of thinking.

The key is to realize that this is what is causing you or your girl difficulties. The problem is that when people, usually our parents and religious leaders, instill this guilt in us, they never instill in us when sexual relations are actually appropriate. While they are usually well-meaning in their intentions, they can inadvertently do a lot of damage.

Well, this is just my opinion, but I see absolutely nothing wrong with sex. Especially if you're in a loving relationship that is based upon mutual respect. Whether you're married, in a steady relationship or whatever, the point is, being a sexual being doesn't make you sleazy. It makes you human. And humans like sex. It's in us. We can't help it. As much as some of the more pious of us like to pretend that we don't need it or want it, we know deep down that we all long for it. There's nothing like a good orgasm. And better yet there's nothing like giving a good orgasm to your lady. This is a good thing and doesn't make you into a pervert or anything. Besides, it would be just plain weird to lock ourselves away from the world and deny that we're adults with sexual needs.

And furthermore, this is true even if you're a religious person. You can have your boundaries and still be a sexual person. You can have sex only with your spouse or significant other, but there's nothing anywhere that says that you shouldn't enjoy it. Or that you should feel ashamed for being a sexual being. This is how you were created and this is one of the reasons why you were created. Sexuality is a gift and if you don't enjoy the gifts you are given, you aren't properly appreciating them.

Of course, I'm not saying to run wild and screw everything or do strange illicit sex acts with people and things who are not interested. That's not what I'm saying at all. What I am saying is that sex is good. Enjoy it. And within the confines of consensual partners, whether it is your wife, girlfriend or whatever, you should have fun. As long as you're practicing safe sex and exercising good judgment, you should feel good about yourself for experiencing one of the great joys of life. It doesn't make you a weirdo or a creep to have an interest in sex. More likely, you'll be looked as more of a weirdo if you show no interest at all. Or if you're disgusted by the sexual act. If you act like this, you'll never get your girl off because she can sense it when you aren't enjoying yourself.

Many people associate repressed thinking regarding sex primarily with females. And with good reason. Women are constantly told from the time they are young girls on up that they shouldn't be slutty, that they need to be modest, that they shouldn't "give it up" too easily etc.... But this happens to men too. We're told to that we'll go blind or grow hair on our palms if we masturbate and various other things that make us feel bad about anything sexual. I have friends who say they feel empty after watching pornography and pretend to have no interest in such matters. Any mention of sex makes them blush. Talk about putting pants on piano legs! If they actually ever had sex, they would probably want to give themselves a bath in disinfectant.

This is absolutely ridiculous. This kind of thinking doesn't make them bad people, but it's not a far stretch to imagine that a person that's this hung-up in regards to sexuality would not be a very good lover. These sorts of people are more likely to "just want to get it over with" rather than take their time to please a woman. It's like they're thinking of it as doing something like taking out the trash or changing the oil in their car. They are glad they did it, but getting there wasn't too much fun. If you're in this category, then maybe you're starting to see the light as to why you have been unable to please your partner.

So how can you overcome sexual guilt?

I've found out that the best way to overcome sexual guilt is to recognize it and stop letting it interfere in your life. When it comes up, just say to yourself that it's just the guilt talking. It isn't really the way things are. It may be hard at first, but eventually you'll overcome these feelings. And the more you do it, the better you'll get at it. And the better sex you have, the less guilty you'll feel about it. You'll also have to take yourself out of the context of sex as bad. You have to realize that sex itself is not bad. It's what people make of it that's bad. Sex is wonderful. It feels good and is truly a gift. However, it's when people misuse it for their own purposes that it turns ugly. When others use it to manipulate or hurt or exploit or even use it against us, this is when it turns into a morality issue. Remember, it's the intention that is important. You have to keep a healthy attitude towards it and look at it for what it is—a physical act. And when this physical act is between two people who love each other, it's even better.

Don't let sexual guilt stop you. There's nothing wrong with sex. It's one of the greatest gifts you have as a human being. The morality of it is in the intention people have when they're engaged in the act. If you only have good intentions and both parties are willing, then you're doing nothing wrong.

If you're going to be a good lover, you have to love sex. You don't have to be a creep or a pervert to enjoy it. You must realize that it is a part of you. No matter how much you try to deny it, you are a sexual being. If you're going to be able to please your woman, you can't be a prude. It's healthy to be a sexual person. In fact, it's how you were born and you are going against nature if you deny this. You have to be able to get down and dirty if you're going to be a great lover. Your girl won't think any less of you for it either. In fact she'll probably be happy that you're finally getting into it and giving her what she wants.

Are you ready to stop feeling so guilty now?

But what if she's the one with the sexual guilt?

As I alluded to previously, sexual guilt is a heavy burden to bear but it's possible that the reason you're having difficulties pleasing your woman is not because of your issues. Maybe it's your girl who is the one who has problems with sex.

If you've found that it's not you that has a problem with sexual guilt, but rather your partner, the best approach you can have is to be patient. Remember, girls have had it drummed into them that they have to save themselves and that they have to protect their virtue from childhood on. Many times, these same ideas carry on into adulthood and throughout their lives. You must be gentle in your approach. Don't look at her hesitations or inhibitions with hostility. Look at them as something that she needs to overcome. It is your duty to help her. Remember good sex is a great way to get over inhibitions and guilt. The better the sex is, the better she'll feel about it. Sure, you may have to gently nudge her, but if you're doing things right, she'll respond appropriately. Regardless of her inhibitions, she is a human and humans love orgasms. You just have to patient and go at her pace. Try something new every now and again. If she resists or complains, apologize and tell her that you were just so turned on that you couldn't help yourself. Eventually, she'll most likely give in to your advances provided you're doing everything right. A great orgasm will do wonders to do away with you or your partner's inhibitions.

Be a gentleman.

It should go without saying that you get what you give out of life. Your relationship is no different. The nicer you are to your girl, the better she'll be to you. If you treat her nice, she'll treat you nice. It's just the way people are. I know there are exceptions to this rule because there are some people out there who like to fly in the face of convention, but we're going to stick to the majority of people here.

A basic fact of life is that if you're an ogre and generally unappealing, you will be regarded as such. Even by your girl. However, if you're a gentleman and do gentlemanly things for her, she'll appreciate you much more. Now, I'm not saying you should be a doormat or be a complete pushover. If you let her walk all over you, she'll have no respect for you either because she'll see you as a weakling. No, what I'm saying is to do nice things for her. Open the door for her. Cook for her. Pump her gas. In other words, do the things that men have traditionally done for women.

Yes, you've heard me. Be a gentleman. Be strong. Be chivalrous. Throw that women's lib business out the window and put her on a pedestal. Treat her like a lady. Do you think that your girl has grown up in a bubble where men don't open doors and buy flowers? Do you honestly think that they want you to treat them like they're just guys with vaginas?

I think you see where I'm going with this.

If you act like a man, she'll treat you like one. If you treat her like a woman, she'll love it.

If you have no idea where to start, here are some tips:

- When you're out on the town, pick up the check.
- Pour her drink.
- Buy her flowers.
- Give her gifts.
- Hold the door for her.
- Open the door for her.
- Cook for her.
- Compliment her clothing.
- Compliment her appearance.
- Offer your coat on cold days.
- If she smokes, light her cigarette.

And so forth.

In my opinion, one of the biggest problems nowadays is that our gender roles have been so watered down by feminism and resentful men who only want to pay women back for lessening their roles that we've forgotten just how to act towards one another. Women love to be treated like women. They love for men to fawn over them. Regardless of our changed expectations regarding gender roles, it's still hard being a woman in this world. It was especially so in the past, that's why all those rules of gentlemanly conduct came about, I think. Men were expected to put women on a pedestal to make up for the hardships that they had to endure what with running a household and childbirth etc... So, why not utilize some of these gentlemanly behaviors now? It will only help your standing in her eyes.

This stuff is fairly easy to do and will reap great rewards. Be a gentleman and she will love you for it. No woman wants to be with some guy who acts like a slob or treats her badly. At least not long term. When you start making an effort and treating your girl like a lady, she'll start appreciating you more. This is not only true in life, but in the bedroom as well.

Look your best.

Looking your best is a very important part of pleasing your lady. If you look like a slob, she'll think of you as a slob. As well you know, slobs aren't necessarily renowned for their lovemaking skills. Sure some of them might be pretty good, but they definitely have a pretty big hurdle to overcome. You don't want this if you can help it.

But she's already your girl, right? So why make the effort?

Well, you want to please your woman, don't you? You want her to be proud to be seen in public with you, don't you? If you have the idea that crappier you dress, the more she'll want to get you out of your clothes, then good luck with that. This is a lazy man's approach and should be avoided. The bottom line is that women like men who dress and look nice.

Also you need to look your best because you don't want to be thought of as a fixer-upper. You don't want to be the guy who would look great if only he knew how to dress. Or even worse, you don't want people thinking that your mother dressed you or that you put on your clothes in the dark. You also don't want to be thought of as a guy who will just wear anything.

I know a guy whose mother has always bragged that he "will just wear anything." To her this means to her that he's easy to please and will wear whatever horrible outfit she buys him. But what it actually means is that he has no concept of what looks good. He truly will wear anything. This is not a good thing. When you're a guy who will wear anything, eat anything or will do anything, it really calls into question your level of taste. And let me tell you, once your girl starts questioning your level of taste, she might just start wondering about your taste in women as well. She may think, if he doesn't care what he wears, then what does that say about me?

The point is that this kind of stuff carries over. So you need to keep this in mind, especially in regards to your clothing.

If you're unsure of what to wear, just look at some men's magazines. Also look at men who are fashionable. I'm not saying you should be metrosexual, but you should make an effort to look nice. You should also dress age-appropriately. If you're a middle-aged guy, you should probably avoid trying to dress like some sort of skateboard punkrocker. Sure this look may be a pretty cool look, but it probably won't be cool on you if you're too old for it. Also, how about asking your girl to help you shop? Ask her to pick out some things for you. She'll love doing this. In addition, it'll give her the opportunity to point you in the right direction so you can finally achieve some level of sartorial splendor.

If you don't know how to start, just start small. For example, women love shoes. In fact, it's one the first things they look at when they look at a man. Knowing this, will you still insist on wearing the old broken down Reebok walking shoes that you grandpa handed down to you? Not if you're paying attention. Buy some nice shoes. Preferably something other than athletic shoes. While there's nothing wrong with athletic shoes, sometimes they can give the impression that you're still dressing the same way you did in middle school.

Just take this same approach to the rest of your wardrobe and you'll be fine. Wear nice pants, jeans or whatever. Then take a look at your shirt. You don't have to spend a fortune, just wear something that gives off the impression that you're a guy who knows how to dress himself. As I mentioned earlier, if you're not sure of what looks good, just look at some *current* men's magazines for tips.

Some of you guys will have a girl who already buys clothes for you. If she does this, wear them. Don't argue. Just wear them because obviously this is how she wants you to dress. Also, chances are she probably has a better sense of fashion than you do. Don't worry about what the guys will say because you're not trying to sexually please them, you're trying to please your lady. And that's what you need to keep in mind.

Hygiene.

It should be quite obvious to most people, but it is surprising to see just how oblivious a lot of men are to their physical hygiene. I'm not sure if it's because their parents were asleep at the switch when they were teaching them their basic human skills or if they're just plain lazy, but a lot of men are just dirty. They either smell bad or seem to have no idea as to how much cologne they should actually be using. Or a combination of both. As you can tell, this isn't going to win you points with your lady. Believe me, they notice when you don't look or smell your best. This isn't good because it's only commonsense that she'll be even more turned on by you if you're clean.

I hope this doesn't insult you too much because that is not my intention. I only want you to look your best. Don't feel too badly if you do fall in the category of the man I'm talking about. It's probably not completely your fault. However, if you remain this way, it will be.

I think to discuss hygiene we need to first define what exactly I mean by this term. What I'm referring to when I use this word is your basic cleanliness. I'm talking about the consideration you give to your cleaning ritual. It's not hard to be clean, so if you just pay attention to what you're doing, you'll be much better off. Some of this stuff will be obvious, but you would be surprised how this basic knowledge has bypassed them.

Your lady will want you to look and smell your best. However, because she knows you're a man, she will cut you some slack, but only so much. You have to essentially be clean. This is the most important thing. We're not talking about the metrosexual topics of moisturization or eyebrow plucking but rather your basic washing ritual.

The biggest thing you need to realize is in regards to your hygiene is that when you're having sex, you will be naked. So you need to look your best naked. This means that you have to keep things clean that you may not have thought about before. When it comes to sex, clothes will no longer be able to disguise any of these shortcomings.

But don't worry, this stuff isn't hard. Here are a few tips.

Pay attention to yourself. Know your weaknesses. If you have dandruff, realize it and use dandruff shampoo. If you have cracked dry hands, apply lotion often. If you have bad breath, brush your teeth more often and use mouthwash. If your lips are always chapped, get some lip moisturizer. Check yourself in the mirror and see that your shirttail is tucked in or that you don't have lint on your sweater. Make this a habit. You don't want to give the impression that you slept in a ditch and dressed yourself in the dark. When you show that you care about your hygiene and appearance, your girl will notice too.

Showering: It should go without saying that you should shower at least once daily. When you wash, work your way downward. Start with your face and hair and work your way down. Be sure to hit the spots most likely create odor. These can be different for different people, but for most people, these areas are: your neck, armpits, groin, behind the kneecaps, feet and ass. If you think for a minute that you may have missed anything, go back and clean yourself again.

Soap: If you're unsure of what kind of soap to use, go with unscented. This way you're playing it safe. Most soaps do smell pretty good—by themselves. However, when you mix these scents with those in your shampoo, deodorant and cologne, you may find yourself an odorous mess. Subtlety is the key.

Your hair: Wash it. Find a good shampoo and stick with it. If you have dandruff, use a dandruff shampoo. If you have oily hair, get a shampoo designed for that and so on. This is simple. Women love clean smelling hair. Keep in mind that your hair can collect odors and smells just like your clothing. If you don't wash it regularly, you can end up with a stinking, lank mop on your head.

Cologne: As I just mentioned before, subtlety is the key. Nobody wants to continue to smell you after you've left the room. Try to pick a scent which smells good on you. Get your girl to help you, if you're unsure. Women love to do this kind of stuff. Also, keep in mind that no one should smell your cologne unless they're within six but no farther than 12 inches of you. If you're unsure of how to apply, just dab a little bit behind your ears. Some people spray it all over them or put it on their wrists. However, this usually creates too strong a smell. Remember it's better that people not smell it all rather than smell it too strongly on you.

Deodorant: Use it. What kind you use is up to you, but preferably an antiperspirant/deodorant works the best towards neutralizing any bad odors. I know there are some men who think that women are attracted to their naturally musky smell, but I wouldn't take this chance. Sure there are some kinky women out there who like this thing, but most women will smell past your pheromones and just think that you need a bath.

Shaving: Most women like the clean shaven look, however some women like facial hair. Go with what your lady likes but with the caveat of whatever you do, keep it neat. A beard or moustache can be a lot of work, so if you go this route, keep this in mind. Make sure it's clean and tidy. Also, if you go the clean shaven route, be sure that that you don't leave any stray whiskers anywhere. Nothing is as unappealing as to see a few stray whiskers under your nose or on your neck.

Teeth: Brush those things at least twice a day. Gargle with mouthwash as well. Also don't forget to floss. Not only will it make you cleaner, it'll also help your teeth. Also, be sure to periodically check your teeth throughout the day to see that nothing is stuck in them. Do this enough and it'll become a habit. Most women like good teeth on a man. If they are yellowed, you might also want to try whitening them.

Hands and fingernails: Keep them clean. Wash them and pay attention to them. If your hands are cracking and bleeding, use more lotion. Make sure your fingernails are clipped and free of dirt. If you have a problem with biting your nails, try to stop. Ragged, chewed up nails are unappealing. Remember you hands are what are going to be touching her. You don't want her to shrink back when you're caressing her, do you? Don't forget your toenails either. You don't want to accidentally cut your girl when you're in bed together.

Most of this stuff is common sense. Just try to stay clean. It doesn't matter how sexy you are, if you're not clean, you'll be a big disappointment to your lady. You don't want her to hold her nose when you're making love to her do you? The more you care about yourself, the more she'll care about you and the more she cares about you, the more turned on by you she'll be.

Exercise.

I know you don't want to hear this but it's true. You need to try to look your best and this doesn't just apply to your clothes. You will also have to work on your body as well. She is going to be seeing you naked after all.

But she loves you for you, right? Not your body. She's just not a superficial girl that is only concerned about appearances, you say. You're probably right. She does love you for you; however, she'll be even more into you if you get yourself in shape. I'm not saying that you should look like Mr. America or anything, but women like men with muscles. And they like them to have trim bodies. You just have to accept this. The more pleasing you are visually to her, the more you'll please her in the sack. It's a very simple concept and you should embrace it. You like to look at fit women, don't you? Why should she feel any differently towards men?

The great thing about it is, once you start getting in shape, you'll probably have more energy and feel better about yourself. This will make you an even better lover because these qualities will contribute to your confidence. It doesn't matter if you're doughy or skin and bones, any physical exercise you do will increase your self-esteem. When you feel good about yourself, she'll feel even better about you. The fact that you're making the effort will also make a positive impression on her. She'll love putting her hands all over a firmer you. When you're having sex, she'll be even more turned on now that she can feel your muscles.

So how do you start? You start. That's what you do. You have to get going. And even harder than this, you have to keep going. You need to pick something and if it works for you, stick to it. You can also improve your diet as well. I'm not saying that you should have a total life makeover, but everyone can make improvements. And sometimes, even a little something can make a big difference. I can't recommend an exercise regimen for you because I don't know your specific needs. I'm also not a doctor so of course, consult your physician before embarking on any exercise program.

Just think of it this way, if you're physically fit, you'll be more sexually fit. The more you appeal to her eyes, the more into you she'll be. And the more into you, she is, the more turned on she'll be. And when she's already turned on, pleasing her will be a piece of cake.

Grooming.

Regardless of the era, one of the most important things that is a turn-on for women is that a man be well-groomed. They expect a man to actually care about the way he looks.

I'm not going to say whether there's any correct way to wear your hair or facial hair, because different styles come and go. However, the most important thing you should realize is that regardless of how you choose to wear your hair, it should be neat. If you couldn't care less about your appearance, more than likely, your girl couldn't care less about you. If you look like a bird has nested in your hair or your moustache has food in it and is growing wild all over the place, don't think that she won't notice. Women do take in these things and they are very important to them. This is why it should be important to you. As I mentioned earlier, she'll cut you some slack just because you're a guy, but only so much.

Remember the more she likes the way you look and smell, the more turned on she'll be. You should also take cues from your girl as to how you should style yourself. If she keeps hinting that she likes short hair on a man and yours is long, chances are she's trying to tell you something. The same thing goes with moustaches and beards. If she says she likes the feel of a smooth face, then take the cue. Most women will let you know what they like but not always in the most direct way.

I know there's the women's fantasy you hear about which entails them liking some greasy, dirty mechanic or rock star, but you need to realize that these are just fantasies. In real life, they would probably scrub these guys and have them tested for venereal diseases before they have sex with them. And if you'll notice, a mutual bath is many times part of the fantasy. Bear this in mind.

So when it comes to your grooming, just pay attention and try to be neat and clean. You girl will appreciate the fact that you care about your appearance. She'll be proud to be seen with you and will not have to make excuses for your slovenliness.

Grooming down there. Should you?

Should you or shouldn't you shave your pubic area?

A lot of guys wonder about this. The ones who don't shave wonder if they should let things remain so out of control down there and the ones who do wonder whether they should continue to make the effort. It's such a hassle for something that is only going to be seen by yourself and your lady. Sure, it looks and feels better, but what does it *really* matter? Why bother?

My opinion is that you should do what you feel like.

Or better yet, you should do what your lady wants.

To many women, this is an important part of their grooming and think that it's only fair that a man should make the same effort. When they're going down on you, they want things to be neat. It's a turn-on for them to see that their man keeps himself groomed down there for them. And also it gives them a better view of your instrument. However, to some women, it's not that important. They could care less. So if she's hairy, she probably won't mind you being hairy so you can both be hairy together. However, if she keeps things neat, she'll probably appreciate the same effort.

So, if you feel like it, do it. If not, don't. It's largely a matter of personal taste. It'll make you look neater for your lady, but it does take some effort. You have to keep it up and shave regularly otherwise, you'll create a considerable amount of discomfort for yourself and your lady what with razor burn and stubble. However, if you feel that this is just one more thing to do and don't feel like committing, don't bother. Just bear in mind that your girl may feel differently.

Wining and dining.

I've mentioned earlier about how you should be a gentleman if you want to please your woman. About how you need to treat her well and let her know how much you appreciate her. It's hard being a woman and you will be well-served to recognize it. But there's another facet of this that will help you out and will ultimately lead to a better sex life between you and your lady. You need to wine and dine her. This is true even if you've been in a relationship for a while.

By wining and dining, I mean that you need to take her out to nice places. Do the things you did when you were first dating. Make her feel special. Women love to go to nice restaurants and cultured events. Sure, they like to kick back with a beer and wings too, but they also love the nicer things as well. This gives them an opportunity to wear their nice clothes and jewelry. It also gives you a good opportunity to shine as well. Your girl will love you in this setting. Sure they love a manly man but this also includes a cultured masculinity as well.

However, it will be good idea to work on your table manners before going to a nicer restaurant. You wouldn't want to spoil the mood by chewing with your mouth open or putting ketchup on your steak (even though you might prefer it this way.) And if her table manners are a little less than desirable, be sure to ignore her misgivings. She'll get better the more often you take her out and see your good example.

So if you want to get on your girls' good side, a nice date and dinner might help. It will not only give you great opportunity to show a more refined, well-rounded view of yourself, it will also give your relationship a different setting. It's great to mix things up sometimes and this will only serve to help your sex life.

Don't bore her.

If your girl considers you to be a colossal bore, then you're going to have a harder time sexually pleasing her than you would otherwise. While orgasms are primarily physical, there is a mental component to sexual attraction as well. If you put her to sleep when you're having a conversation, then there's a good possibility that her libido will be drowsy around you as well.

But how can you tell that you're boring her? It's simple. Is she participating in the conversation? Is she giving you one word answers? Is she falling asleep when she's talking to you? Do you have to keep repeating yourself to her when you're telling her a story? If any of these situations is occurring, then it's a good possibility that you're boring her. This is a fairly easy fix though. All you probably need to do is modify your topics of conversation. You'll probably want to avoid telling her the minute details of what you had for lunch or scene by scene synopses of your favorite science fiction movies. Also avoid talking about sports because most likely she doesn't care.

But what else are you going to talk about?

It's easy. Her. You talk about her. You ask her about her day. If she's like most women, most likely she'll be her own favorite subject. And if you think this is particularly one-sided, you're right. However, it'll lead to other topics as well. She'll talk about what she's interested in. You can interject your own stuff in there wherever you see an opportunity. Just don't lead the conversation with it.

So, if you want to please your woman, just don't bore her. Talk about stuff she likes to talk about. Save the sports and movie analysis for your buddies. If you don't, most likely you're going to get more than your fair share of opportunities to do this.

Safe sex.

Unless, you've been living under a rock all your life, you should know that it's always a good idea to practice safe sex. The use of condoms and birth control are very important to prevent both sexually transmitted diseases and pregnancy. If you're in a committed relationship, then the safe sex option is a matter between the two of you. Just bear be honest about your sexual history with your partner. You should also insist upon this honesty from your partner as well. If you have any doubts, insist that you both get tested for any undiagnosed STD's.

When nothing works.

Let's say that you've done everything right. You've been a gentleman. You've treated her like a queen. Your technique is excellent and you've done nothing wrong. However, she's just not getting off.

So, what did you do wrong?

Well, if you've done everything right, you've done nothing wrong.

Sometimes, despite your best efforts and intentions, you will not be able to get your girl off. Sometimes she'll be unable to focus enough to have orgasm. She may have had a bad day at work. She may have a lot on her mind. Maybe there are family problems going on. Whatever the case, sometimes it just isn't going to happen.

So what do you do?

First off, you need to give her time. If, after a prolonged sexual encounter, she doesn't seem to any closer to finishing than she was, gently ask if she's close to orgasming. She should tell you if she is or isn't. If she isn't, keep doing what you're doing. Do not stop until she lets you off the hook even if you know it's not going to happen for her. Most women will let you know that they're not going to be able to do it and will tell you to go ahead and finish. If she does this, make sure that you do finish. Do not decide that the gentlemanly thing is to pull out and wait until she's ready. She'll take this as insult because most likely, even though she isn't up for an orgasm, she is still enjoying the sexual attention. It feels good and if you just pull out, it'll almost seem like you're not having a good time. This will only hurt her pride. You always need to finish. Especially when she tells you to go ahead and orgasm. Remember what I said about how you should wait until she orgasms before you do? This is the one rare exception. But remember that this time she is giving you permission to go ahead. That is the difference.

Sometimes this same situation happens earlier in the process and usually for the same reasons. During foreplay. Despite your best efforts, she just can't get into it. If this happens, don't get upset. It's not you. Just politely suggest that maybe the two of you should try it later when then mood is better. Don't force her to have sex with you when she is not in the mood. Most likely she only went along with trying to get things going because she cares for you. You should care enough for her to pick up on when things aren't working out the way they should.

Don't do anything to hurt her pride or self-esteem. Just be nice and don't get huffy. She'll probably be glad you suggested this if things aren't progressing smoothly as long as you do it in a nice way. It's better that no sex act happens than for a bad one to proceed. However, if she wants to keep at it, just try to keep doing everything right and hope for the best.

The moral of the story is that sometimes things just aren't going to work out for a variety of reasons. When this happens, know when to call it a day and try again later. As long as you're nice and let your enthusiasm for her show, you should avoid any of the problems that may occur if you persist when the mood isn't right.

Conclusion.

So are you ready to please your woman? I think so. It's really not that hard of a thing to do if you know the basics. Remember you're just trying to get the place where you can give her an orgasm. How you get there is unimportant. Just so she's pleasured. People are different and different things turn them on. Your girl is no different.

The great thing is that once you get comfortable with getting your girl off, it'll be that much easier because your confidence and enthusiasm will grow. Since confidence and enthusiasm are such huge parts of what it takes to be a great lover, this only makes sense.

Your girl is counting on you to get her off. Sure she can always use a vibrator, but as you yourself know there's nothing like the real thing. She'll love it when you can consistently give her an orgasm. She'll look forward to having sex with you and will know that she can count on you to give her what she wants and needs. People love orgasms and women are no exception. Just think about the power you have to make her happy. Don't forget that a sexually satisfied woman is much easier to get along with too. If this isn't motivation enough for you to improve your sexual prowess, than nothing is.

So get out there and give it to her. Once you hit your stride, she won't be able to get enough. This much you can be assured of.

Printed in the United Kingdom by
Lightning Source UK Ltd., Milton Keynes
142460UK00001B/66/P